Basic
Radio Control
Flying

Other titles in this series include:

Building from Plans   David Boddington
Installing Radio Control Aircraft Equipment   Peter Smoothy
Setting Up Radio Control Helicopters   Dave Day
Flying Scale Gliders   Chas Gardiner
Operating Radio Control Engines   David Boddington and Brian Winch
Covering Model Aircraft   Ian Peacock
Moulding and Glassfibre Techniques   Peter Holland

Basic
Radio Control
Flying

David Boddington

ARGUS BOOKS

Argus Books
Wolsey House
Wolsey Road
Hemel Hempstead
Hertfordshire HP2 4SS

First Published by Argus Books 1989

ISBN 0 85242 980 0

Phototypesetting by Ethnographica, London N7
Printed and bound in Great Britain by
William Clowes Ltd, Beccles

Contents

Chapter 1
Introduction

Learning to fly a radio control model aeroplane must rank as one of the most satisfying and enjoyable periods of any hobby involvement. It is also one of the most challenging times and can be frustrating and discouraging unless approached in a realistic, knowledgeable and logical manner. Without proper guidance during these initial stages the chances of obtaining success are very limited and it is all too easy for the newcomer to become disillusioned before he has experienced the joys of accomplishment.

Whether the guidance comes in the form of verbal and physical assistance, or from the written word alone, we believe that this publication can help you in your preparation for—and attainment of—flying radio control powered model aircraft. It will assist you in preparing yourself, the model and ancillary equipment before visiting the flying site, it will inform you of the behaviour when you arrive and take you through the flying exercises to enable you to become a competent pilot.

How do we define Basic R/C Flying? It is that period of learning to fly which takes you past going solo (surely one of the high spots of all experiences!) to the point of becoming a competent pilot. Competency, with an R/C model aero-

plane, can roughly be considered as being able to recover the model from any position or attitude that it may attain—accidentally or otherwise. For example, if the model inadvertently enters a spin then, given sufficient height, you know how to recover and are capable of taking the necessary recovery action. Being able to fly the model to this standard *almost* assumes that you can also fly the model accurately in normal flight—this is certainly a prerequisite for competency. Accurate flying and an understanding of basic aerodynamics are also necessary for achieving a high standard of consistent landings. Every flight must end with a landing, or a crash, so learning the finer skills of circuits and landing is an absolute essential.

Although much that is written here is equally applicable to powered models and gliders we have concentrated on the former. Gliders require specific launching techniques (from hill sites, or by a towline or bungee from a flat field) and are outside the scope of this publication. No doubt a forthcoming handbook will deal with this subject.

Join the Modellers

Most of the major Western and Eastern bloc countries have governing bodies

The thrill of your first solo flight is one of the highlights of our hobby. Typical of basic trainer models, the 'Instructor' is a high wing stable model.

to organise aeromodelling competition events and co-ordinate the activities of the hobbyists. Because these bodies are comprised of active and enthusiastic aeromodellers they have one major aim and interest—to promote the hobby in the widest possible sense. They are there to help YOU and the more members who join the parent associations the more they will be able to do for all aeromodellers. We would certainly recommend any newcomer to the hobby to join their national governing body; your local model shop should be able to give you details of how to get in touch with them.

To give a couple of examples of what the associations can do for you:–

The AMA (Academy of Model Aeronautics —USA) has a total membership of around 130,000 and this is large enough for them to carry some political 'weight', even in a country as large as the USA. Throughout the world modellers are having problems in finding suitable flying sites and the AMA have a scheme (costed in tens of millions of dollars) to develop five regional sites across the breadth of the country. These will not be just barren flying areas, but fully developed areas with hotel/motel facilities, meeting areas, camping locations and a golf course—truly forward thinking and a sign of the increasingly important part that our hobby will take in leisure time of the future. An impossible dream? Based

Governing bodies of aeromodelling, such as the British Model Flying Association and Academy of Model Aeronautics coordinate hobby activities.

on the present membership it represents less than $200 per head—not so impossible!

One important aspect of the work of the BMFA (British Model Flying Association) is to provide the R/C Achievements Schemes for power and glider flyers, to encourage them to reach given standards of flying ability, and to have this recognised by proving it to a local examiner. About 3,000 people in Britain have reached either the A Standard, which equates to a safe solo standard of flying, or the B, which is normally required if you intend to fly at a public display. Both levels include simple flight competence sections and also questions on the Safety Code, which is in the handbook which every member receives, and which is packed with information about insurance (the Society's £1,000,000 third party policy covers all members), the Achievement Schemes, noise, BMFA organisation and how you can help, and basic details of R/C frequencies and contest rules, which let you get still more from model flying.

Although it has only been possible to mention two of the many governing bodies similar projects and assistance will be organised by other associations and these, normally, will be affiliated to the FAI (Federation Aeronautique Internationale) the world organisation dealing with the aviation sports.

Addresses

AMA, 1810 Samuel Morse Drive, Reston, Virginia 22090, USA.

BMFA, Kimberley House, Vaughan Way, Leicester LE1 4SE.

Clubbed

Although not all clubs are affiliated to the governing body there are still obvious advantages in joining a model aircraft club. There will always be experienced modellers on hand to give you help and advice and you will be unlucky indeed if you do not benefit from the assistance they can give you. The skill of flying radio-controlled models is not easily acquired, and the beginner needs all the help he can get. Joining a club and getting the help and support of experi-

Model clubs attract a wide variety of modellers, young and old, and types of models.

enced model flyers is the quickest road to success —and the cheapest! This handbook is designed to provide the novice with a programme of learning by which he can avoid pitfalls, acquire good habits and check his progress. Though it has the club member in view, it should be helpful to those who, from necessity or choice, are going it alone, as it sets out what there is to be learned, and a well-tested way of going about it. We have included a separate item to assist the 'lone ranger'.

We have not tried, in detail, to help with building, equipping and maintaining the airframe; there are other sources for that kind of information. We do see the need, however, for a concise basic course in the actual handling of the model in the air.

A very sketchy introduction to Theory of Flight has been included, because some learners benefit from insight into the reasons why the aircraft does this when the pilot does that. An understanding of rigging and trimming is really essential for those who wish to get the best handling from their model.

We have noticed that pupils are often inhibited by the fear of looking clumsy or stupid in their early efforts. Have no fear—model fliers have all been through those traumatic early stages; they know it isn't easy and they are much more ready to sympathise than to sneer. The beginner will forfeit sympathy, however, if he over-compensates by becoming 'big-headed', or if he ignores the simple demands of safety and courtesy which club flying entails.

A few dos and don'ts:—

DO   Learn and observe the Club's rules.
Show thanks for help and encouragement.
Help in general Club chores (eg moving the strip, maintaining the club-room and equipment) and especially help in any area where you have special skill or resources. Try to avoid wasting your instructor's time; be sure you and your model are ready to go when he is ready to take you.

Advantages of belonging to a model group or club are the help and training you will receive and the sharing of a common interest.

... and they say pigs can't fly. After you have learned the basics of flying you can progress to many types of models.

DON'T Walk heedlessly across the landing-path.

Choose the wrong pit area if you arrive first. (See the circuit diagram).

Fly over the pit or spectator area.

Switch on without frequency clearance.

Start your motor when something tricky (eg the first flight of a Class 1 scale model) is going on.

Hog the frequency peg when someone else wants to fly on your channel.

Borrow tools, etc., and forget to return them.

... or alone

Without the benefit of a club to help your training you must negotiate for a flying area (as large as possible, clear of trees and well away from habitation) and find a like-minded person to give you moral and practical support. Wherever you fly you *will* need insurance and one source of this is ASP Readers Services, PO Box 35, Wolsey House, Wolsey Road, Hemel Hempstead, HP2 4SS. Write for details of this scheme which covers all forms of aeromodelling in the U.K.

There are legal limitations on flying model aircraft. For instance, in Britain when they weigh in excess of 5kg ready to fly, less fuel, they are subject to flight limitations. However, it is unlikely that any training model used in the initial phases will weigh as much as 11¼lb—if it does, you should certainly be a member of a club, or group, and they will be able to advise you on procedures.

Whichever way you decide to proceed with learning to fly radio control model aeroplanes, we wish you every success and hope that this publication will help to make the path a little easier and the progress more enjoyable.

Chapter 2
What type of model?

Go into six different model shops and ask proprietors for the ideal training model and you would be lucky if you didn't come out with six different model aircraft. There is no such thing as THE perfect training model, any more than there is such a thing as THE ideal wife—or husband—there will always be a certain amount of argument on the best type of trainer and the best method of training. What we can do here is to point you in certain directions, AFTER you have decided on the most applicable type of training and other constraints such as costs, transportation and flying sites. Which route you take will depend on your particular conditions and preferences.

Alone, or with an instructor

In the previous chapter I emphasised the advantages of belonging to a club or group with good facilities and a fully operative training scheme. Unfortunately, all potential R/C model fliers are not in the position of participating at a club due to the locality or because the club flying times are not suitable. Where the new enthusiast is forced, by circumstances, to go it alone (or, at the best, with an inexperienced assistant) the type of training model will be different from that of the trainee with an instructor

constantly at his elbow during the critical learning phases. Where YOU are the one that has to make all the decisions during the flight you will want a model that gives you the maximum time to allow you to arrive at the RIGHT decision. Having an instructor prepared and able to take over control of the model at a second's notice—when you are in trouble—allows for a rather more advanced trainer to be used right from the preliminary stages.

To build or to buy

Dyed in the wool, traditionalist modellers who have been involved in the hobby for many years may abhor the introduction of Almost-Ready-To-Fly (ARTF) models. These examples of modern technology and manufacturing developments are total anathema to the modeller brought up on a diet of balsawood chippings and the aroma of dope and balsa cement. For them, you must have built the model—with a reasonable degree of blood, sweat and tears—as well as had the pleasure of flying the finished product.

We live in a busy and hectic age where there are many demands upon our leisure time and we do not always have as much time to spend on our chosen activities as we would wish. If *flying* an R/C model is, to you, going to be the

11

most enjoyable aspect of the hobby then by all means purchase one of the modern ARTF kits—or even a fully built conventional model, there is usually a reasonable selection available in model shops. Having learned to fly with an 'instant' model you may well find yourself drawn further into the hobby and positively *want* to build your own models—perhaps even design them. Although the flying and building aspects of the hobby can be treated totally separately it is almost certainly true to say that the more you put into it, the more you will get out of the hobby. It will be satisfying to be able

to say 'look, I am flying that model up there' but it will be even more satisfying to say 'look, I am flying MY model up there'.

Of course, there are not only the extreme alternatives of building from scratch (from raw materials and the drawing) or purchasing a near complete model: kits are available for very many training models in varying degrees of prefabrication. Some provide merely the plans, instructions and the correct quantities of the various materials with little preforming carried out. Others, naturally more expensive, will have all the parts

For modellers with little spare time to spend on building models, the ARTF (almost ready to fly) approach allows more of your leisure to be spent actually flying.

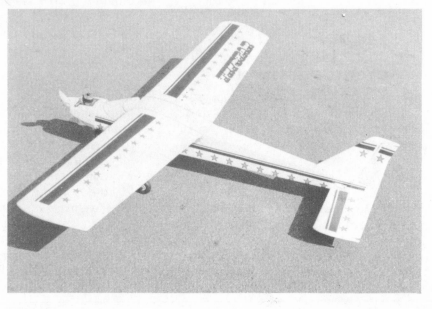

No one can deny that the ARTF models are attractively finished. Most are I.C. engine-powered, but some have electric motors fitted.

pre-cut and, in some cases, pre-assembled. In other words, there is a full range of products available to allow you to choose the amount of effort and participation in preparing the model to the stage of being ready to fly.

For those of you wishing to follow the traditional route there are further Handbooks in this series which will prove invaluable for the beginner. These are *Building from Plans* and *Installing Radio Control Aircraft Equipment, Operating Radio Control Engines* and *Covering Model Aircraft*, which will also be of great assistance to the newcomer to R/C flying.

What size?

As with many of the problems we face in life, there is no simple answer and compromise has to play a major part. All other things being equal, large training models have much to be commended; they are easy to see, and therefore to maintain orientation, and better suited to a wide range of weather conditions.

However, all things are not equal and the costs involved will, alone, restrict the overall dimensions of the models and engine sizes to moderate proportions. Transportation is another factor that will probably limit the sizes of models; trying to carry an eight foot wing span trainer in a small family car may not be practical. It is regrettable that more model clubs do not have a comprehensive training scheme where training models are supplied as part of the overall scheme. In this way it should be possible to utilise larger designs which, under the guidance of qualified instructors, would be both safe and more suitable for the ab-initio trainee. Using standard designs, powered by economic spark ignition engines, a pupil could be trained to solo state much as a car driver is taken to driving test standard by a commercial driving school.

Many trainer models, kit and plan designs are based around .20cu.in. engines. Economics influence this choice to a large degree but it also represents the smallest models that can reasonably be expected to perform adequately in the variety of weather conditions we are likely to experience. If we are prepared to wait for nearly ideal flying conditions it is

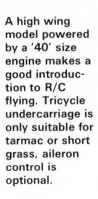
A high wing model powered by a '40' size engine makes a good introduction to R/C flying. Tricycle undercarriage is only suitable for tarmac or short grass, aileron control is optional.

possible to learn with smaller models (even electric powered or powered glider types) but continuity of training is important and few of us have the patience to wait for those idyllic conditions. Selecting a model designed for the '30' to '40' range of engines allows us to go a little larger without the costs escalating unduly.

With low cost two-stroke engines now being available in these ranges the difference in costs should not exceed £20.00 and it does give an opportunity for those wishing to use four-stroke engines to fit a '35' or '40' engine to these models. The cost of the radio control equipment remains the same for each type.

So, with these parameters decided, let us take a closer look at the individual designs.

Basic trainers

High or shoulder wing models offer the best prospects for the majority of beginners to R/C flying, i.e. those with no, or minimal, organised instruction and the luckier ones who can take advantage of a club training programme. Rightly or wrongly, most beginners want their model to 'look like a real aeroplane' and many trainers have therefore been designed as cabin models in the style of 'Cessna' and 'Piper' aircraft. Aerodynamically, a shoulder wing design, without any cockpit area, would be just as suitable. The purpose of the fuselage, in our case, is to accommodate the engine, fuel tank and radio equipment and to support the wings and tail surfaces at the required position. Any other considerations, apart from structural integrity, are purely cosmetic.

Much nonsense has been written about wing aerofoil sections, particularly with regard to trainer and sports models. With built-up wings, i.e. those with open areas between the structure, the covering material naturally 'sags' between the rib stations and the aerofoil section of the rib is not faithfully maintained. In truth, for basic training models, we are not looking for a super efficient wing section; it is more important for the builder to be able to achieve a light, robust and TRUE wing. A wing with a flat-bottomed section of proven performance is easy to construct (built directly onto the building board) and is strong enough to service normal knocks and hard landings; the small price to pay for these advantages is a slight 'ballooning' tendency (the nose of the model rising after a build-up of speed during flying). For this reason it is important not to overpower the model and risk excessive speeds.

For the keen builder, who prefers the challenge of constructing open framework airframes, many Vintage designs are suited to the purpose of an ab-initio trainer. Originally designed as free flight models, they are stable and slow flying. With radio control fitted, usually limited to rudder, elevator and engine throttle control, they become guided free flight models with ample time for the operator to make the necessary control inputs. Left to their own devices—when properly trimmed—they will fly in a perfectly satisfactory manner and, therefore, if panic does set in, the pilot only has to release the controls and the model (given sufficient height and time) will recover itself. For these reasons vintage designs, or similar replicas, are particularly suited to the beginner who has, by force of circumstances, to go it alone. Do not be misled by the apparent flimsy appearance of this type of model; soundly constructed and covered with nylon or a heat-shrink fabric they are tough and resilient.

Light weights and wing loadings give slow flying speeds which, in the event of a crash, involve lower impact speeds and

When you have a qualified instructor with you during training you can start with a low wing, four function design. More responsive and less stable than a high wing design, it will suit a young novice with quick reactions.

the flexible nature of the structure often allows the stresses to be absorbed without damage. However, the slow flying speeds and limited 'penetration' into winds does mean that patience is required to wait for the right conditions for flying.

At the other end of the scale we have the low wing, aileron equipped model which is altogether faster and more responsive. With a qualified instructor as your constant companion, to take over control to get you out of the 'impossible' positions you will undoubtedly get yourself into, this type of model is certainly a possibility. It is probably more suited to the young budding flier, where reaction time is lower (and the experience

Ensure that your launch assistant knows exactly what to do; he must only launch – with a firm, level throw – when you are ready.

with computer games will have an indirect benefit to operating an R/C transmitter). There are also 'natural' fliers who seem to take to R/C flying without any real difficulties; if their potential can be assessed early on they would also benefit from starting with a more advanced type trainer. One distinct advantage with low or mid-wing trainers featuring symmetrical wing sections (or near so) is that they can be flown in a wider range of wind conditions.

Alternatives

Electric-powered models, particularly in the ARTF market, are becoming increasingly popular. Superbly presented, packaged and finished, the plain truth is that few of these products are suitable for the absolute beginner. For volume sales reasons—or that would seem to be the reason—many of the electric ARTFs are scale models. With those based on high wing prototype training aircraft (Cessnas, Pipers etc.) you have a degree of chance in succeeding to learn to fly; with WW2 offerings (Mustangs, Zeros, etc.) you have no chance. One or two models *specifically designed* as trainers and not based on full-size prototypes do give you a better chance of learning something about R/C flying before the demise of the model, but the models are frequently too small to be considered as suitable trainers for the average modeller. Perhaps this situation will change quite rapidly— the Far East manufacturers were never slow to fill potential markets—but until this takes place you would be better advised to keep to the larger, conventionally constructed models powered with IC (internal combustion) motors.

Although the majority of R/C model aeroplane enthusiasts learn to fly with conventionally powered fixed wing models there is a further option. Gliders, either operated from a slope (hillside) or launched from a flat gliding site, can be

Not many of the electric powered ARTF models on the market are suitable for basic trainers – the 'stick-plane' shown above is one of the few exceptions.

quite suitable for the learning process and an 'intermediate' possibility favoured by some is the powered glider. With the latter type of model the motor—not normally fitted with a throttled carburettor—is used to get the model to height and after the engine has cut the model is treated as a glider.

R/C equipment and engines

It is not the purpose of this handbook to deal in detail with radio equipment or engines. As mentioned previously, these are the subject of separate titles in this series. However, for the uninitiated, a brief word about the requirements may be of assistance when making initial purchases.

Except for gliders and powered gliders (where two-function radios may be adequate) it would be a sound investment to purchase an R/C outfit with five or six functions. It is likely that only three functions (rudder, elevator and motor)

A buddy box system, with the instructor's and the pupil's transmitters connected by an 'umbilical' cord, is an ideal way of learning to fly. It allows the instructor to take back control at any moment.

operation. If you are serious in your intentions to make R/C model flying your hobby, then replace the dry battery power with rechargeable nicad cells. This option is normally available when purchasing the equipment. Frequency wavebands allocated for R/C model aircraft use will vary from country to country, although European countries are tending to standardise on the 35 MHz (35.00 to 35.24 in Britain). America uses channels (spot frequencies) on 53, 72 and 75 MHz frequency bands. Always check with your governing body regarding frequency allocations as these tend to change from time to time. If you are, or have, joined a club check first with their frequency recommendations—and the transmitter mode (1 or 2) they use. When flying training is to be undertaken under the guidance of recognised instructors the advantages of using a 'Buddy-box' system cannot be over-emphasised. With the instructor's transmitter (the master) connected to the student's transmitter (the slave) by an 'umbilical' cord it is only a matter of the instructor releasing a button to regain control. Naturally, transmitters must be compatible for this system to work and the R/C

will be required in the first instance, but it will not be long before the additional functions will be required for more advanced models. Many of the 'economy' outfits are supplied for dry battery

There are two principal ways of holding the control sticks on the transmitter, between the finger and thumb (left) or with the thumbs on top of the stick (right). Choose whichever method is the most comfortable and natural to you.

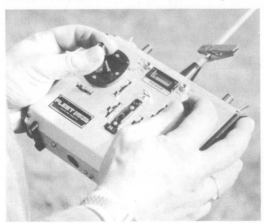

equipment must be designed to incorporate this feature. Regrettably, all too few do have this training facility as a standard part of the transmitters; it would improve training efficiency enormously if the Buddy-box system was generally more available.

Well over 90% of the IC engines used in normal sized R/C model aircraft (up to 5kg in weight) are glow motors. These engines are started by energising a glow plug (similar to a spark plug but featuring a spiral wound element which glows red hot when an electric current is applied). Once running, the electric power source can be disconnected and the engine continues to operate. Two-stroke engines are the most common but, due to environmental noise considerations—

and pleasant operating qualities—the four-stroke motor has gained tremendous popularity over the last few years. For the beginner the four-stroke engine has the *disadvantages* of greater complexity and higher price; it has the *advantage* of sounding less frenetic when the model is in a dive and may, therefore, cause less panic to the flier.

All plans and kits normally specify the engine range suitable for the model. It is not necessary to go to the top of the capacity range: a plain bearing, economy motor in the middle of the quoted range should be quite adequate.

Diesel engines, in the smaller capacity engine range, are preferred by some modellers. They do not require a starter battery—operation is purely by compression ignition—and are equivalently powerful to the glow motor. Because they have two adjustable controls, the needle valve and the compression screw, the engines take a little longer to get to know and to operate correctly. In some non-aeromodelling circles the diesel is also considered as smelly and dirty!

Spark ignition engines are only available in larger capacities and are not generally used on trainer models.

'Aerobat' is a suitable choice as a first model for a pupil/instructor training system, or as a second model for the lone flier.

Vintage style models such as the 'Super 60' shown here make excellent trainers because of their slow flying and stable characteristics.

How many wheels?

One final consideration which will affect the model design selection process— the flying site. Where you will be operating from smooth mown grass, or a hardstanding, then a tricyle undercarriage equipped model will be the number one choice for the beginner.

The tricycle undercarriage will help the model to track straight on take-off and, if the nosewheel is made to contact the ground *after* landing, it will prevent the model from leaping into the air again if there is excess speed at the touch-down.

For grassed flying sites, with no mown strips, it will be impossible to carry out take-offs from the ground and it will be necessary to hand launch the model. In this case there is no point in having a tricycle undercarriage and a two wheeled type with the wheels well forward (as often found on vintage designs) will allow the model to land without—if you are lucky—tipping over. As the un-prepared flying sites often go with the lone flier it is even more sensible for the independent operator to opt for the vintage style model when learning to fly. The slower flying qualities make it easier to hand launch and the landings, in the rough grass, will also be slower and less hard.

You should take pride in the building and finishing of your models, but do not spend too much time on the decoration as it may be even more heart rending if the model does crash.

Chapter 3
Simple theory of flight

Now there's a misnomer! The theory of flight is anything but simple and has been the subject of many hundreds of books. Even books on aerodynamics relating specifically to aeromodelling have tended to be rather learned publications and not easily digested by the average R/C flier. But is it necessary to understand aerodynamics to fly radio control model aircraft? Strictly speaking, no! However, a knowledge of the fundmentals of flight will help the beginner to R/C flying to avoid dangerous flight conditions—inadvertently spinning a model, for instance. Knowing the cause and effect of controlling the model will help you to fly correctly and will also help you to prepare and trim the model to make it fly as accurately as possible—the rest will be up to you.

Within the confines of one chapter it is only possible to skim the surface of aerodynamics and our simplified explanations must be generalised. We strongly recommend that any modeller progressing into more advanced areas of R/C model aircraft, particularly if you wish to design your own models, should purchase the publication *Model Flight* by Martin Simons and published by Argus Books. This excellent book looks at how and why flight behaviour can be influenced and explains—in simple language—the basic aerodynamic factors affecting flying models.

Before you move rapidly onto Chapter 4, thinking that the remainder of this chapter need not concern you, just remember this. When we are unfortunate enough to crash a model it is important to know why it has crashed. As the reason for it is often through aerodynamic causes we must be able to understand the rudiments of aerodynamics to be able to avoid such errors for a second time. There is no doubt that such words as 'aerodynamics'—even 'theory' —tend to frighten modellers away— perhaps this chapter should just be called 'What makes an aeroplane fly'.

Invisible lift

Of the four forces acting upon a powered aeroplane three, weight, thrust and drag (the resistance of the model to the air) are readily understood. It is the fourth force, lift, that seems to create 'bogies' in the minds of modellers. Ask any young schoolboy what keeps an aeroplane in the air and he will confidently tell you that it is the engines pulling the aircraft through the air! When you then ask how a glider manages to stay in the air— sometimes for many hours—they are at a loss to explain this magic away.

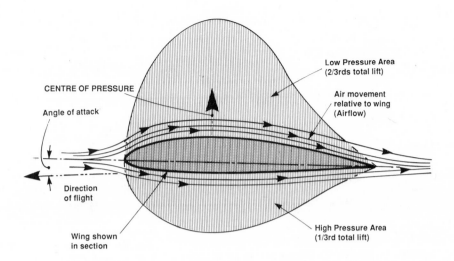

Fig. 3.1 Lift on the wing is created by the wing moving forward at an angle of attack (angle of wing chord to the actual direction of flight).

CENTRE OF PRESSURE

Angle of attack

Direction of flight

Wing shown in section

Low Pressure Area (2/3rds total lift)

Air movement relative to wing (Airflow)

High Pressure Area (1/3rd total lift)

Aircraft (by definition, heavier than air machines) need an upward force to keep them 'airborne'. This 'lite' force is provided by the supporting surfaces (wings) at right-angles to the direction of flight. Because such lifting surfaces are positioned at an angle to the normal airflow and because the surfaces are, for efficiency, streamline in section, the on-coming air (which is fluid) separates at the leading edge of the wing. With a shorter path for the air to travel along the lower surface it arrives at the trailing edge before the flow along the upper surface.

In an attempt, by the lower flow, to rotate around the trailing edge a vortex is formed. In turn, this vortex accelerates the upper surface flow so that the time taken for the airflow over the upper and lower surfaces is equal. The higher speed of the flow over the upper surfaces produces a lower pressure and it is the difference in the upper and lower (higher) pressures that creates the lift.

About two thirds of the total lift is generated on the top surface and the magnitude of lift is related to the speed of the model through the air and the angle of the wing (angle of attack). However, if the angle of attack is increased excessively the airflow can no longer follow the upper camber, and as it detaches itself from the surface, a stall (loss of lift) occurs.

The theoretical point through which the forces on the wing act is called the *centre of pressure*.

If all this sounds a trifle confusing it is sufficient to remember that lift, all other things being equal, is a product of speed and angle of attack. It follows that if the airspeed of the model is low we must increase the angle of attack (increasing the nose-up attitude) to maintain flight.

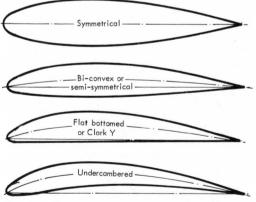

Fig. 3.2 Some common wing section types used in models, Symmetrical is suitable for full aerobatic designs, bi-convex for aerobatic sports models, Clark Y for basic trainer (vintage style) and the undercambered aerofoil for very slow flying (non aerobatic) types.

21

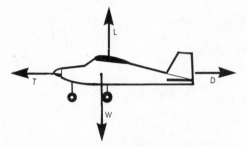

Fig. 3.3 Forces acting upon an aeroplane.

Taking this to extreme, excessively slowing down the model and trying to compensate by increasing the angle of attack (with up elevator) will result in a stall, i.e. a loss of lift, and consequently loss of control. Stalling has caused the demise of more aeroplanes, model or full-size, than any other cause.

Forces acting on an aeroplane

In straight and level flight, these forces are adjusted so that the Thrust is equal to the Drag, and the Lift is equal to the Weight (which acts through the centre of gravity—CG).

In a turn, the vertical component of the Lift decreases. As the Weight is un-altered, the aircraft will lose height unless the lift is increased.

Lift can be increased by:

(i) Opening the throttle. The Thrust will now exceed the Drag, and the airspeed will increase. The faster you go, the more lift.

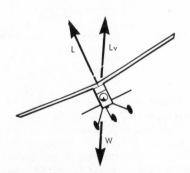

Fig. 3.4 Forces acting in a turn.

Fig. 3.5 Increasing the angle of attack gives more lift and drag.

(ii) Giving Up elevator. This increases the Angle of Attack of the wing, which gives more Lift. Unfortunately it also causes more Drag, so the airspeed will be reduced, unless more throttle is used.

Climbing. To climb, the throttle is opened, increasing the airspeed and hence the Lift. The nose is allowed to rise (see under 'Pitch Stability' below); this introduces an upward thrust component and the aircraft climbs.

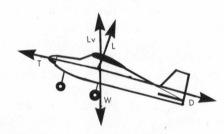

Fig. 3.6 Forces acting in a climb.

Gliding (i.e. descending with the throttle closed). When we reduce the power the nose drops ('Pitch Stability' again). The Angle of Attack decreases, decreasing the Lift, and the aircraft descends. Drag also is reduced, so the aircraft maintains its airspeed.

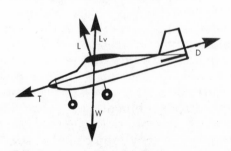

Fig. 3.7 Forces acting in a dive.

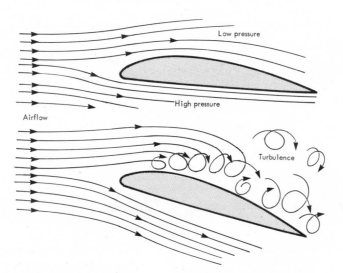

Fig. 3.8 Airflow follows the wing section smoothly at low angles of attack (top). If angle of attack is increased excessively the air cannot follow the airfoil contours and breaks away from the surface – causing loss of lift and a stall.

Stalling, as we have previously stated, is a sudden loss of Lift and increase of Drag, caused by the airflow over the top of the wing breaking away when the Angle of Attack becomes too high.

Note that the Stall is caused by the high angle of attack and not by low airspeed. It is possible to stall the wing of an aircraft at high airspeeds, if sufficient control force is available, by suddenly increasing the angle of attack. But stalls are much more likely to occur at low airspeeds, where the angle of attack tends to be progressively increased to obtain enough lift to maintain flight.

Spinning. When an aircraft reaches the stalling angle of attack while violently yawing, the 'inside wing' will stall sooner and much more sharply than the other, so that the wing retaining some lift will 'spin' the aircraft around its vertical axis. So long as the yaw is retained this motion will continue, the aircraft being unable to gain airspeed or to equalise the lift on the two wing-halves. To recover, the yaw must first be removed and then the angle of attack decreased to below the stalling point. (Most trainer models will recover as soon as the rudder is centralised, but height is needed to pull out of the ensuing dive).

Effect of controls

The effect of rudder on an aircraft with dihedral is two-fold. First, the tail is pushed to one side by the reaction of the airstream on the rudder, so that the aircraft is not flying along its fore-and-aft line, but sideways. This we call 'yawing', and the angle between the fore-and-aft line and the direction of flight is the 'Yaw Angle'.

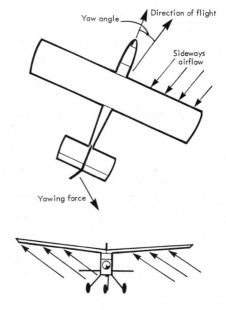

Fig. 3.9 Model yaws, initially, when rudder is applied.

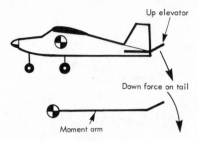

Fig. 3.10 Elevator action rotates model through centre of gravity.

Second, the 'Dihedral Angle' (i.e. the angle by which the wing-halves slant upwards from the fuselage) gives the 'upwind' wing an effectively greater angle of attack, so that the lift on that wing is greater, causing the aircraft to roll in the direction of yaw (i.e. to 'bank' in that direction).

Once the aircraft is in a bank, the Lift has a horizontal component which causes it to move in a circular path. (Note that in a high-wing aircraft the rolling force is assisted by the fuselage shielding the downgoing wing from the sideways airflow.) Thus a model can only be effectively steered by rudder alone if it has generous dihedral or a high wing position, or both.

The effect of elevator movement is to produce an upward or downward force on the tail. This force tends to rotate the

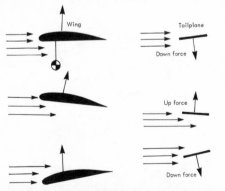

Fig. 3.11 Tailplane, set at negative incidence, creates a slight down force in level flight (top), an up force with higher angle of attack (centre) and greater down force in dive (lower).

aircraft about the Centre of Gravity, causing the Angle of Attack to increase or decrease. Note that if the throttle setting is not changed, the end result of using elevator is to change the airspeed, not the height, of the model. Hence we arrive at one of the fundamental principles of low-power flying.

ELEVATOR controls AIRSPEED
THROTTLE controls HEIGHT.

Stability

The trainer is designed so that any disturbance from straight and level flight will produce an opposing force to restore the status quo. These stabilising forces have to be provided in three dimensions:— Pitch, Yaw, and Roll.

Pitch stability. Our designer has provided two stabilising factors:—

Tailplane ('Stabiliser' in America); in a trainer, the wing is rigged at a positive angle of incidence relative to the tail-plane. In straight and level flight the tailplane is producing a slight downward force to compensate for the effect of the forward CG.

When the angle of attack of the wing is increased, the tailplane also acquires more angle of attack and now produces lift, exerting a leverage about the CG to bring the tail up again.

Similarly, when the wing angle of attack is reduced the tailplane takes up a negative angle relative to the airflow and produces an extra downward force, bringing the nose up again.

Pitch and airspeed

The stabilising force produced by the tailplane increases with the airspeed, so that there is only one speed, i.e. the correct cruising speed, at which the stabilising forces exactly balance the aircraft. At higher speeds the download on the tail will be increased, causing the aircraft to 'zoom', as we quaintly put it. As the aircraft climbs, however, it will lose airspeed and seek to return again to level flight at cruising speed.

Conversely, if the airspeed drops below cruising speed the tailplane will not be able to provide enough downward force to balance the aircraft, so the nose will drop and the aircraft will go into a shallow dive, picking up speed and thus assisting the stabilising force on the tailplane.

These effects produce a kind of stability in airspeed, with the model trying at all times to maintain the normal cruising speed. (That is why it doesn't pay to fly a trainer at full throttle, when the excess airspeed will require excessive down elevator to prevent climbing). This type of stability is at its most useful in landing approaches, when the model should automatically correct a dangerous low airspeed by dropping its nose.

Directional ('Yaw') stability

This is produced by the Fin (i.e. the fixed vertical surface at the rear of the airframe). The Fin reacts against the sideways airflow, producing a force tending to realign the aircraft with the airflow.

Note that if the fin is small in relation to the side area forward of the CG, its stabilising force will be feeble. On the other hand, if it is too large it may override the control force of the rudder, and it may also tend to stabilise the aircraft in a spiral dive, with unfortunate results. The size of the fin is therefore an important consideration in trainer design.

Roll stability

Two forces stabilise the aircraft in roll:
Dihedral We have seen before that the dihedral angle causes a rolling force when the aircraft is yawed. When the yawing force is released, however, the

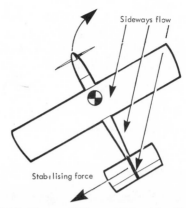

Fig. 3.12 Yaw stability produced by fin.

two wing-halves revert to producing equal lift. But because of the dihedral angle, the lift of the lower wing has a greater vertical component than that of

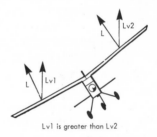

Lv1 is greater than Lv2

Fig. 3.13 Roll stability produced by wing dihedral.

the upper wing-half, tending to roll the aircraft upright again.

Pendulum effect The high wing position of the trainer places the centre of pressure well above the CG. The aircraft is in effect 'hanging' from the centre of

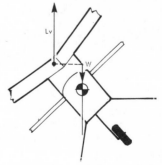

Fig. 3.14 Pendulum stability produced by low C of G.

pressure so that in a bank it has a tendency to roll upright again, assisting the force provided by the dihedral angle.

Note that when the aircraft is inverted, the roll stabilising forces become the opposite; i.e. de-stabilising. Therefore a trainer will roll much more easily from the inverted than from the upright position.

Design considerations

A trainer is designed to have positive stability about all three axes, Vertical, Horizontal and Longitudinal. The controls have to overcome the stabilising forces in order to make the model obey the pilot's commands. Therefore the model prefers to fly itself and is sluggish in response to the transmitter. This is well suited to the beginner, who has not yet learned to be sensitive in control; he also appreciates the fact that the model will not destroy itself unless he gives it grossly inappropriate commands. It does have disadvantages, the main one being that a model which is very stable in pitch reacts sharply to airspeed changes and can easily get into the 'zoom-stall-dive-zoom' syndrome which is the great bugbear of the student pilot. This, together with poor penetration and the inertia effects described below, makes for difficulties in windy conditions.

Engine thrust-line
Downthrust The trainer's high-wing position sets the Centre of Drag well above the engine thrust-line, and that gives rise to a nose-up couple, whose force increases with the thrust. Furthermore, extra speed will mean more drag, which will also increase the couple.

At cruising thrust and speed, the couple is balanced with the other stabilising forces. At greater speed and thrust we must have a nose-down balancing force which also varies with the thrust. This is achieved by inclining the thrustline downwards, which produces two compensating effects; one, a downward component of the thrust, and two, bringing the thrustline nearer to the Centre of Drag.

Sidethrust This is necessary because of engine torque. The force exerted by the crankshaft to turn the propeller is accompanied by a reaction tending to roll the aircraft in the opposite direction i.e. looking from the rear, to the left. The only way we can produce an opposite rolling force is to yaw the aircraft to the right, and we do this by offsetting the thrustline to the right. Thus we obtain a balancing force which varies with the thrust, tending *roughly* to balance out the torque.

Effect of speed It will be noted that while the aerodynamic stabilising forces vary with airspeed, the forces which arise from engine offset vary with engine speed and are unaffected by airspeed. Thus Thrust offsets are at their most effective when the throttle is open and the airspeed is low, e.g. in take-offs or overshoots—and that's exactly when we need them. On the other hand, excessive use of offset thrust can cause trimming problems, so it's not a case of the more the better; one must try to get the compromise right.

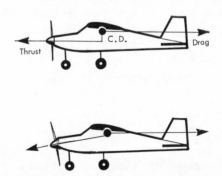

Fig. 3.15 **Engine down thrust brings line nearer to centre of drag.**

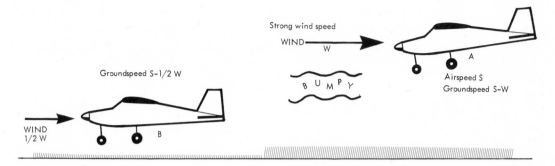

Groundspeed S–1/2 W

WIND
1/2 W

B

Strong wind speed

WIND——W

A

Airspeed S
Groundspeed S–W

B U M P Y

Fig. 3.16 Effects of wind gradient, ie. lessening of wind speed near the ground.

Wind-speed and inertia

'Ballooning' As soon as the beginner flies in any considerable wind, he encounters the obvious phenomenon of the model rearing up as it turns into the wind and the less obvious (but more dangerous) converse of a rapid loss of airspeed as she turns downwind. Modeller's Lore is usually silent about these—admittedly often controversial—phenomena, the reason being that our wisdom is usually based on full-size flying manuals, which do not mention them. The fact is that they affect full-size aircraft much less than models, because (i) the big ones travel normally at airspeeds much greater than normal windspeeds, and (ii) a full-size aircraft cannot turn at anything like the rates that are normal for a model.

The phenomena are caused by the varying inertia of the aircraft as it turns. The inertia varies because it is a function of the groundspeed, and not of the airspeed. (If you don't believe that, try flying into a telegraph pole upwind, and then downwind!)

Wind gradient has caused the demise of innumerable models—and a good many full-size aircraft too. One again it is caused by changes in wind velocity, but as we are dealing with aircraft near the ground these changes can produce a dangerous situation.

A fresh to strong wind loses considerable speed near the ground, both through friction and through turbulence ('gustiness') caused by obstructions (e.g. trees) or uneven ground.

In the diagram, the wind at point A may have twice the speed over the ground that it has at point B. The inertia of the approaching aircraft does not allow it to adjust immediately to the rapid decrease in the velocity of the air in which it is flying. (To put that another way, the inertial force will tend to maintain the groundspeed at a constant value, whereas to maintain airspeed the groundspeed will have to be increased). There will also be unpredictable variations in airspeed due to gusts. Thus a pilot landing in windy, turbulent conditions will need to allow a respectable safety margin over his usual approach speed. Again, the effect is much worse for models than for full-size aircraft.

Chapter 4
Preparation for the flying site

Irrespective of the model you are using to learn to fly there are a number of check exercises and preparations to carry out before you make for the flying field. In fact, you have already commenced that preparation by reading and—hopefully—understanding the basic aerodynamics.

If the lessons of control surface inputs have been inwardly digested' it will also be realised that it is essential for all the flying surfaces on the model to be true and straight if it is to fly accurately.

Any warps (twists) in the wing, tailplane or rudder will make it impossible to correctly trim the model for all flight situations. For instance a warp in one wing panel may be counteracted by applying aileron adjustment on the opposite wing, but this will only be effective for a given speed. At speeds lower or higher than the trimmed speed the warp may be more, or less, effective than the aileron trim. It follows, therefore, that everything possible should be done to check for warps and misalignments on the model and corrections made. Some people are gifted with an excellent ability to 'eyeball' the model (looking at it from various angles) and notice anything wrong with the flying surfaces. Others of us have to do it by using visual aids and taking measurements—see sketches.

Very many models have been crashed through having an incorrect balance point (often, and incorrectly, called the Centre of Gravity, or CG. This is the point at which there is a *three* dimensional equilibrium). Too often a rearward balance point is accepted by the novice, inevitably resulting in a model which is uncontrollable in pitch (elevator). A balance of the model *slightly* ahead of the design position is acceptable, rearward of the specified balance point—NEVER.

Having a model that you can rely on is half the battle won in learning to fly. Relying means, in this case, a model that is built truly and soundly, an engine that will keep running and throttle smoothly and a radio installation equipment that will not fail. Having another experienced modeller check the model over is the surest way of finding any faults; if this is not possible make certain that you have read all the relevant instructions concerning the preparation of the model, the installation of the engine and radio equipment—and complied with them. Check the operation of the radio (do all of the control surfaces move in the correct direction?) with and without the engine running. Run the engine until it will operate happily at all throttle settings and set the throttle servo linkage so that

Fig. 4.1 Check thoroughly all dimensions on the model relating to alignment of the flying surfaces. A model which is misaligned can never fly accurately over the full speed range.

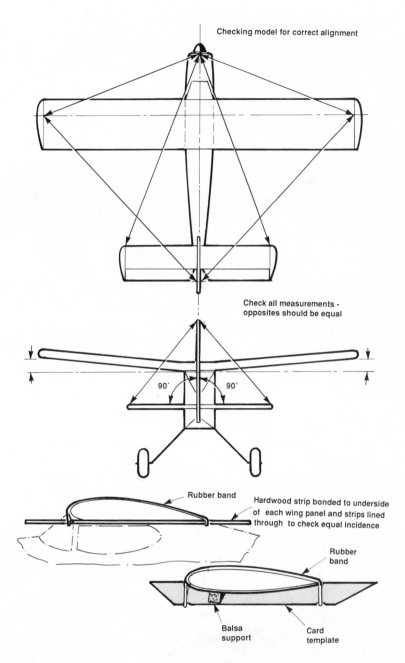

Checking model for correct alignment

Check all measurements - opposites should be equal

90°   90°

Rubber band

Hardwood strip bonded to underside of each wing panel and strips lined through to check equal incidence

Rubber band

Balsa support

Card template

you have a reliable 'idle' with the transmitter stick fully back and the trim forward—movement of the trim lever should then result in the engine stopping.

Use the period between completing the model and waiting for suitable flying weather—often a frustrating month or

so—to familiarise yourself with the transmitter. Once the model is airborne there will not be any time to take a quick glance at the transmitter to find out where the trims are, your eyes will be firmly fixed on the aircraft. View the model from all angles and, with the radio

Check all controls thoroughly before attempting to fly, and have a check list to remind you of your pre-flight checks.

switched on, make imaginary corrections to turning, climbing and diving. In particular, get used to controlling the model from a head-on position where the directional control—left and right—become apparently the reverse of when the model is going away from you. I say 'apparently' because the model is reacting in exactly the same way to movements of the control stick, the reversing is due to you standing in a different relative position to the model. Some fliers get used to this situation by imagining themselves sitting in the 'cockpit' of the model (when the controls are continuously relative to the 'pilot') or, more prosaically, by working on the principle that if the wing on *your* left is low the

The author explaining to TV star Paul Daniels the operation of the transmitter before giving him his first taste of R/C flying. Because of his natural attributes he only needed dual instruction for a very short period before going solo.

control stick must be pushed to the left to correct it—with the model coming towards you. Whichever way you decide to adopt it is vitally important to get used to this situation. Trying to watch the model by looking at it over your shoulder —so that it is facing the same way—is doomed to eventual failure and is a bad habit to get into.

Field equipment

Frustrations come in many forms but few exceed the situation where you arrive at the flying field, with the model and with perfect weather conditions, only to find that you have forgotten a vital item of equipment.

With all of the pending excitement of learning to fly it is all too easy to overlook the preparation of auxiliary equipment, tools and spares that will be needed at the flying field. Ideally, one should have an inventory list, pinned to the field box in a clear plastic wallet, to remind you of the items to take with you.

Field boxes come in all shapes and sizes and degrees of sophistication. They range from plastic buckets to 'baby boxes' and through to purpose-designed commercial units. You will eventually decide yourself which items you consider 'essential' to have at the flying site, but here is a preliminary list to start as a basis.

1. Complete model, transmitter, aerial and frequency flag.
2. Clean and fresh fuel, filler bottle or pump, primer bottle, fully charged glow battery, glow clip, cable and plug testing facility.
3. Spare glow plugs, propellers, fuel tubing, starter, finger guard or 'chicken stick'.
4. Rubber bands—if required.
5. Tools, including plug spanner, prop nut spanner, pliers, wire cutters, screwdrivers, modelling knife, cyanoacrylate adhesive, pins, spare nuts and bolts.
6. Pad and pencil—for making notes about model trim.
7. Detergent squeeze bottle, cleaning rag and paper towels.
8. First aid outfit.
9. Liquid and other refreshments.

Adrenalin time

On the morning of the great day—your first flying experience—check that the model has been properly charged and give a final check of the controls on the model. Make sure you are sensibly clothed—for hot or cold conditions— and have a pair of sunglasses with you. A final check of the weather forecast, to see whether conditions are likely to improve, and you are ready for the off!

Chapter 5
Field etiquette and layout

Whether you need to know and exercise any field etiquette will depend on whether you are flying alone or at a club flying site. If you are entirely on your own, at your own flying site, then you only have yourself to worry about—plus any interested spectators who might turn up to enjoy the entertainment! As a member of a flying group, with a communal flying area, it is rather different, and here you have to follow certain procedures.

When you arrive at the flying field and have parked your vehicle in the designated area, walk across to the pits area (where the models are parked) and introduce yourself to some of the members. They will, no doubt, introduce you to one or more of the committee members who, in turn, will explain to you the rules and regulations at the flying field. For obvious safety reasons it is necessary to have rules in operation at any flying site and they are not intended to be unduly restrictive, simply to make flying a safer and more pleasurable undertaking. By now, you should have received a copy of the club constitution and regulations so you should be pre-warned about many of the local conditions and rules. There may be restrictions on when and where you can fly. These may seem irksome but there will

be good reasons for them, probably to keep favour with any local inhabitants and not to overstay our welcome.

Once you have made your contacts, found out about any training schemes in operation and been taken under the wing of an experienced pilot, it is time to fetch your model. Do have your mentor cast his professional eye over the model and do take any criticisms as they are intended—to be helpful.

Providing everything is in order, or can be safely corrected on site, you are ready for the first steps into the thrills of R/C model flying.

All alone

But what if you are one of those modellers who may be living in a far-flung rural area, with no option but to learn to fly without any more assistance than a sympathetic (but unskilled) friend and this handbook to guide you? It is not intended to depress you unduly but it must be said that your chances of success are not too great. Providing you are prepared to persevere you will make it, eventually, but it may result in a little heartbreak—and broken models—along the way. The real problem is that there is no way of easing into the learning to fly situation. Once launched—and it may not even be the best of launches—you have to start learning immediately and, by the end of the flight, have learned sufficient to be able to get the model down again. A tall order! However, be of good cheer, it can be done—the author did it, there was no one else around to proffer any advice. And that was in the days when R/C equipment was a lot less sophisticated, or reliable, than it is today.

When you are operating on your own it is vital to take a thorough look at the site and get your bearings so that, when you are flying you know automatically which way you are facing. This may seem an unnecessary action—believe me it is not. When you are concentrating 100% on the model your peripheral vision is limited to an indistinct background. Being able to immediately recognise the area of background is important, as it will help you to keep check of the progress of the model. So, just stand in the position you will eventually be flying from, mentally plan the landing circuit you will be making (as described in the next chapter) and take note of the geographical features in the background at various points of the circuit. You will need some specific 'bench marks' to act as key points for flying the circuit.

Having a clear idea of your actions and reactions is important at all flying sessions and it is vitally important for the first flying session. Planning the procedures carefully will help to restrict the chances of failure; you will know how to react to given situations and have positive aims to achieve. Without planning you are likely to be so amazed when you see the model flying that your mind will go into neutral and you stand there, mesmerised by the model, until something untoward happens and it is too late to take corrective action.

Never attempt to fly the model totally on your own, the assistance of a calm, responsible and practical helper is essential even though he may not have any personal knowledge of aircraft. You will need someone to hold the model when the engine is being started, to help you during the range checks of the radio equipment, to launch the model and to give you moral support during the flight. He may not be able to give you advice on the actions to take, but he can be reassuring and confirm such facts as the direction of flight of the model, whether the engine has stopped, how long you have been flying and the relative position of the model to obstacles. You will also require someone to share in your elation on a successful first flight or, if things do not go quite so well, to help you analyse the problems that occurred and what actions you took—or failed to take.

No modeller can plan ahead for desirable weather conditions and you must have patience and wait for a day when the wind conditions are suitable, i.e. a wind strength of not more than 5 mph or, ideally, totally calm conditions. With a no wind situation you have the advantages of being able to land in any direction in an emergency and a constant speed of the aircraft over the ground for a given air speed (in windy conditions the model will have a greater ground speed down wind compared with upwind and this can be confusing to the novice who wrongly tends to relate these movements to the model's air speed.)

When the great day does finally arrive do carry out all of your pre-flight checks thoroughly, promise yourself to keep to the pre-arranged programme and do not be tempted to fly unless everything is working 100%. Take your time over the flight preparation: there will be a strong urge to get the model started and into the air but a steady, cautious approach will help to keep you calm and unruffled.

Chapter 6
First flights and
flying exercises

Because much of this chapter will be dealing with training flights under tuition let us first deal with the lone hand and how he can cope with that nerve-wracking first flight. Actually, it is one of the most exciting experiences you can have and if it is successful—or even partially successful—the sense of achievement is tremendous. It will be forever etched on your memory and will make all the trials and tribulations well worthwhile.

You will note that the position in which the pilot stands is somewhat different from that taken up by the pilot under instruction. There are good reasons for this, not the least of which is that it is easier to control the model in the initial stages if you are standing immediately behind it as it climbs away. As there will be no other modellers or 'planes to worry about when you are flying you are not going to inconvenience anyone else, or be a danger to other persons. Where there *are* other models being flown at the same time considerations dictate a different siting of the pilots and a need to always fly in front of you. On your own, the last thing you want is to have to move around with your transmitter or to have the task of learning the basics of flying made any more difficult. However, enough of the theorising, let us get onto the flying.

Circuit pattern

Landing circuits are normally flown in a left-hand direction, not because they are

Concentration and satisfaction. To be in full control of the model throughout the whole flight is a most enjoyable experience.

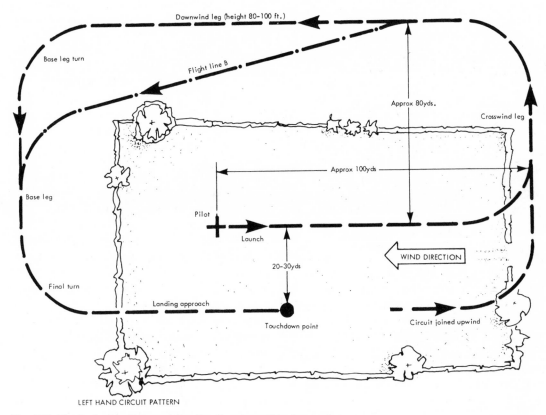

Downwind leg (height 80-100 ft.)

Base leg turn

Flight line B

Approx 80yds.

Crosswind leg

Base leg

Approx 100yds

Pilot

Launch

WIND DIRECTION

Final turn

20-30yds

Landing approach

Touchdown point

Circuit joined upwind

LEFT HAND CIRCUIT PATTERN

Fig. 6.1 Typical circuit layout for the 'lonehand' trainee pilot.

easier to fly than right-hand patterns, it is simply a throw-back to full-size training where the student sits on the left-hand side of the aircraft! However, unless there are flying site restrictions to dictate otherwise (tall obstructions on the left-hand side, for instance) it is as well to stick to convention, as at least it removes one further decision to be made. The accompanying sketch shows the general layout of the circuit pattern and you will notice that the pilot does not stand in the centre of the field but more to the left-hand side and down-wind. Try to keep the memory of the landing circuit firmly in your mind at all times.

For the first flight you will not go straight into a landing circuit; you will want to get the 'feel' of the model for four or five minutes before attempting a

landing—not too long or you may find your concentration beginning to lapse. Assuming that field conditions are not suitable for a take-off, your assistant must launch the model for you when, and only when, you are ready. The model must be launched firmly (tell him to ignore the fact that the model is 'pulling' out of his hand) directly into wind and in a level attitude—not upwards, as the aim is to build up the model speed above the stalling speed as rapidly as possible. Be ready to make any corrections to the rudder or elevator but avoid over-correction—small transmitter stick movements should be sufficient if the model has been accurately built and the balance point is correct. Fly straight ahead, climbing gently, until the model has reached a safe height (100 feet) and try a turn to the left to bring it back towards you. Throttle back until the model is no longer climbing and practise turns to the left and right; be prepared to correct the turns if they become excessively steep—over 45° angle of bank. Keep the model within reasonable range at all times, for when it is at too great a distance it will be more difficult to see and there is a greater delay between seeing what the model is doing and taking corrective action.

Throttle the engine back even further and note what happens. Unless corrective action is taken with the elevator the model will descend. Apply a little up elevator and the model will maintain height but will slow down. This is one of the most essential lessons to be learned for achieving accurate landing approaches, i.e. speed of the model is controlled by elevator (down elevator for increased speed and vice-versa) and the rate of descent (distance covered across the ground to touch-down point) is controlled by increasing or decreasing the engine speed. If this chapter does no more than to drive home this misunderstood fact it will have been worthwhile!

Having become accustomed, in some small way, to the flying characteristics of the model and corrected the trims on the transmitter to get the model to fly reasonably straight and level, it is time to contemplate the landing. Do not aim to land off the first circuit but use this as a practice approach and to get used to the rate of descent at various throttle settings. Join the circuit in an upwind direction, in front of you and at a height of about 80–100 feet, with the throttle at a medium position to maintain height. About 100 yards upwind commence a 90° left-hand turn onto the cross-wind leg; you will not have to fly straight on this leg for long before commencing another 90° left-hand turn onto the downwind leg. This leg is flown parallel to the landing approach and at a distance of 80 yards

from the pilot, trying to keep a constant height and speed. Continue down wind until the model passes you and is 50–60 yards further downwind, reduce throttle to commence a steady descent and make a turn to the left. The length of the base leg will be sufficient to allow for the final turn to bring you directly into wind and for the model approach to be about 20–30 yards downwind of you. The model should be slightly descending throughout the base leg and final turn; adjust the rate of descent (throttle) so that the start of the landing approach is not too low— say 40 feet high. Get the model lined up into wind, with the wings level, as soon as possible so that you can concentrate on making elevator and throttle corrections and only have to make minor rudder movements. Keep the model steadily descending until you are ten feet or so off the ground, open up the engine and commence another circuit—beware of over-relaxing after the concentration of carrying out the practice circuit, you must be in control of the model at all times. The only difference between the next landing circuit and the previous one is that the throttle trim should be pulled back to allow the engine to be stopped completely—you will have to keep a little more throttle stick on to compensate for this and avoid pulling the stick right back until you want to 'chop' the engine.

Fly the circuit as before and when you are satisfied with the landing approach continue to make a touch-down—do not worry if the model is going to land a bit further up the field than you planned, or is further away than the suggested 20–30 yards, the important consideration is that it is directly into wind and at a steady rate of descent, i.e. that you have not got to make any violent last-minute corrections. At a height of about 10 feet cut the engine (it will take a little time to stop completely) and ease on a little up elevator to slow the model down towards

Your helper should launch the model reasonably fast, and most importantly, level to the ground with wings horizontal.

the landing speed. The aim is to level off a foot or so above the ground, gradually increasing the elevator to maintain that height until the model sinks gently onto the ground.

Eliminating the faults

Fine in theory, you might think, but it doesn't always work out in practice. If we examine some of the most common failings it may assist in recognising the potential faults and help you to avoid them. Without any doubt the two major problems experienced by learners are disorientation and over-control. Disorientation—recognising the direction and attitude of the model—will only be overcome by experience, on the ground and in the air and by keeping your eyes continuously on the model. Applying the correct rudder control when the model is coming towards you might also be related to disorientation and this too, will only be conquered by good preparation and recognition of the problems. Over-correction, excessively coarse movements of the transmitter control

sticks, often results from panic reactions where there is a delay in recognising the attitude of the model and taking the necessary corrective action. For example, the pilot feeds on left rudder stick and, apparently, nothing seems to happen. Not realising that the control will take time to become effective (the rudder will yaw the model before a bank is initiated) the pilot gives more rudder movement and suddenly, from no turn at all, the model is now banking steeply. A pause whilst the brain engages and tells the thumb to move to the right and full right is now needed to straighten up the model from a screaming left-hand dive. Turning an R/C model aircraft is similar to turning a car, you don't wait until the corner is there before taking any action, the turn is initiated as you approach and feed the turn in gradually. Thinking ahead and making smooth, proportional, stick movements is the only way of overcoming over-control. Remember, if you do get into a difficult situation the first action should be to close the throttle, level the wings and correct the dive or climb with gentle use of elevator.

Circuit corrections

I suppose the most terrifying happening during circuit flying, model or full-size, is to have sudden engine failure. In calm conditions simply aim to land the model somewhere near the centre of the field with a minimum of turning to achieve this. With a light wind blowing (and you should not be flying in a stronger wind) it is still preferable to land into wind providing that you have sufficient height to carry out the necessary turns at a reasonable height. You will have to think quickly and plan your modified circuit rapidly. If you are in any doubt about lining up for the landing into wind with time to make the final elevator and rudder corrections (say 20 feet high) you would be advised to land downwind and concentrate on height, speed and directional control.

A common fault during the downwind leg is to converge towards the landing areas instead of keeping a parallel course—see flight line B on sketch. This will entail excessively sharp turns onto the base leg and/or the final turn and is likely to affect the control of the landing approach due to continuing rudder control being required. Having to turn tightly near the ground is always fraught with dangers; seeing the ground apparently coming up to meet a wing-tip causes instant panic reactions and it is unlikely that you will recover from the situation and be able to settle down to a sensible approach. If at any point during the base leg, final turn and landing approach you feel that the positioning is radically wrong, it is safer and less agonizing to abort the landing and make another circuit.

Although it is highly desirable to get the model lined up into wind in good time on the final approach it does not mean that the rudder control can be totally ignored during this final phase.

Slight deviations in direction can be expected, especially as the closing of the throttle and reduction of engine torque effect may cause the model to drift to the right. There is a risk of concentrating so much on the elevator and throttle that the rudder control is overlooked.

Another fairly common fault is to aim the model too much towards yourself on the landing approach with almost mesmerising results. A model that is coming straight for you can be quite unnerving and for the inexperienced it is difficult to know whether to make corrections to the model or to run. Alternatively, the model may pass close by at head height causing a difficult transitional period between the model coming towards you and, very rapidly, going away from you. Keeping the model some distance away for the landing prevents any sudden changes of visual attitudes.

Judging the stalling speed of a model —the speed at which the aeroplane ceases to fly—is no simple matter and yet it is all-important for good landings. You can practise stalls and recoveries (nose down, build up speed, ease back on elevator) at a safe height but this does not give the same impression as the model flying closer to you from a side view. During the final phase of the landing there is the danger of applying too much elevator, slowing the model excessively and reaching the stalling speed at an embarrassing height of around ten feet. There is no recovery from such a situation as this—the nose will drop and the speed cannot be built up before contact is made with the ground. Experience is, again, the real answer to judging the correct approach speed and until this is gained you should concentrate on making a steady, constant descent and holding the model a foot or two off the ground until the speed decreases sufficiently for it to settle down. Small and smooth movements of the elevator stick are the order of the day.

Conclusions

You will tend to be more 'unflappable' in your circuit and landing flying if you have a clear impression of the route you should fly. Practise circuits and landings assiduously and as you become more experienced you can try right-hand circuits and landings in stronger wind conditions.

Don't be over-ambitious, or become over-confident; make your progress steadily and concentrate on accuracy before attempting more difficult conditions. Keep a routine until you become more proficient, trying to maintain a consistent circuit pattern.

In a discourse about landing an R/C model aeroplane you might expect to read rather more about the actual *flying* of the circuit and the *techniques* of landing. However, the planning and preparation, including mental preparation, are more than half the battle and, providing your manual dexterity and co-ordination are reasonably good, the physical flying is a matter of steady progress. Of course, a little luck will not come amiss and it can make all the difference between damaging a model and getting away with a poor arrival (crash?) unscathed.

DUAL FLYING EXERCISES

No amount of studying written wisdom will teach you to fly a model; there is no substitute for practice. Try to get in as much flying time each week as you can, as a long lay-off can make you feel you've returned to Stage One.

It is useful, however, to study the notes for the appropriate Stage or Stages, and if possible go through them with the instructor, before each flying session. (You will notice that the Notes for the early stages are directed primarily to the Instructor, and those for the later stages to the Pupil). If you both know in advance what you will be trying to achieve when the model gets airborne, you can make better use of the time.

Transmitter position

You will note that, with the exception of the overhead eight figures, the pilot position is outside the circuit and that all flying is carried out in front of the pilot and instructor. This is done for safety reasons. If, as has been done in the past, pilots all stand by the landing strip (and behind the model for take-off) there are real risks of accidents occurring with models landing amongst pilots and helpers. It *is* more difficult to take off a model when it is being viewed from a position where it is not so easy to judge whether the model is facing directly into wind. However, it is not that much more difficult to learn from these positions and, with the help of your instructor, is

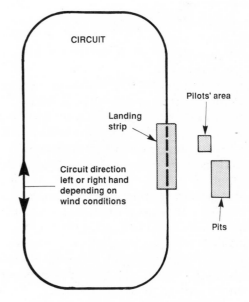

Fig. 6.2 Circuit layout for a club flying field — note that the pilot stands outside the circuit.

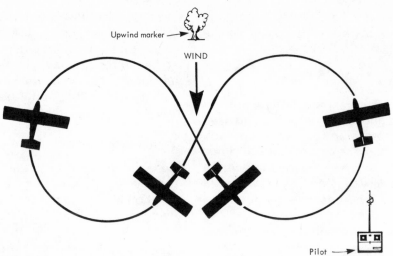

Upwind marker →

WIND

Pilot →

Fig. 6.3 Upwind eights.

something that should be mastered from the beginning—you will have to fly with this layout at many events. You may still see some experienced (or, at least, modellers of long standing) R/C pilots who will dash to the opposite side of the landing runway so that they can land 'over their right shoulder'. This is a bad habit to get into as it is dangerous and disconcerting to the other fliers. For similar reasons it is vital, once left-hand circuits and landings have been mastered, to practise right-hand circuits until you are equally competent with this direction. The reason for left-hand circuits being the norm was mentioned previously, it is purely a convention and there is no advantage over right-hand (clockwise) types. Whether a left or right hand circuit is flown should depend on the prevailing wind conditions and the flying field layout.

Overhead eight figures should be practised at a time when you have the flying site to yourself, or fellow fliers will allow you to have a few minutes flying on your own. Although, in theory, when following the flying exercises you should not fly overhead, or behind you, there will be times when things get a little out of hand and the model will indeed do just

this. You *will* make turns in the wrong direction on occasions and then it is important to realise the error and take corrective action. Disorientation occurs rapidly when flying directly overhead and you must learn to recognise the appearance of the model if this happens accidentally; flying the model purposely overhead is the only way of doing this. It also encompasses the other great disorientation factor—flying towards yourself.

Upwind eights

This pattern is flown at cruising revs, using rudder only. The aircraft is kept upwind; the safest place for a beginner, and the pattern avoids flying the aircraft towards the pilot, which causes disorientation. The turns are made as wide and gentle as we can reasonably make them.

The instructor trims the aircraft, identifies an Upwind Marker at least 100 yards away, and demonstrates the pattern, showing that:—

Only very small and occasional stick commands are needed.
As soon as the aircraft reacts, control is slackened.

Over-control causes a dive; recovery causes a zoom.

A dive is counteracted by opening out the turn; a zoom by turning—we do not use elevator or throttle at this stage.

While the pupil tries this out, the instructor makes any small throttle adjustments necessary to regulate height. The first few lessons can be tiring for the pupil; the Instructor should take over every now and then to enable him to relax.

Once the pupil has grasped the pattern and can execute it continuously without strain (usually after two or three flights) he can proceed to Stage 2.

Stage 2
Steeper turns

This is the same pattern, speeded up by steepening the turns. By cruising at a little more throttle, and using a little UP elevator, we can make these tighter turns without losing much height—but we soon find that the aircraft will not maintain a turn of more than about 30° bank without beginning to dive.

Once the turn has become steep more UP elevator will not stop her diving; it merely tightens up the turn. The aircraft gathers speed and then when we come out of the turn we get into a dive/zoom syndrome. We must therefore learn to prevent that dive developing, which we do by taking the turns in three stages:—

(i) Initiate with rudder
(ii) Keep the nose up with elevator
(iii) Slacken off rudder as the turn steepens.

Some pupils soon get the hang of this, and begin to control the aircraft in a more confident and positive way. Some go at it very gingerly, hardly differentiating between Stage 2 and Stage 1. At this stage, confidence is more important than precision; we want to be sure that if

(or rather when!) the pupil inadvertently 'overcooks' a turn, he will take the necessary corrective action without going weak at the knees. Many therefore need encouragement at this stage to fly with dash and spirit. It helps in this to keep plenty of height in hand throughout.

Some find the spiral dive appalling, to such a degree that they persist in losing orientation and have to be rescued many times by the Instructor. A little patience here will pay off. It does no harm to encounter orientation problems early on. The only real answer is to identify with the aircraft, following its flight pattern as if you were in the cockpit, so that you know at all times which way it is turning and which way you now want it to go. This is hardest to do when the aircraft is flying straight at you, which is the case we tackle in Stage 3.

Stage 3
Overhead eights

This exercise underlines:—
(i) The effects of wind, especially the difference between airspeed and ground-speed;
(ii) The effects of disorientation, as the aircraft flies towards and overhead of the pilot;
(iii) The problems of the downwind sector.

Repeating these '8s' should help the pupil to realise that the attitude of the aircraft (nose up or down) is the best indication of its airspeed. An aircraft can stall going downwind at a high ground-speed, a factor that must be grasped before one starts practising base-leg turns at a low altitude.

As we noted at the last stage, the problems of orientation never disappear until the pilot is mentally following the aircraft through its flight-path, rather than trying to 'compute' its needs from his remote position. This comes with practice, and lapses of orientation may happen even to an experienced pilot when for some reason he takes his eyes off the model. The pupil should therefore not be disheartened when he finds himself often turning the wrong way— he should be learning, however, to recognise this early and correct it quickly.

Such an error can be embarrassing when the aircraft is downwind of the pilot, and the wind is strong.

Disorientation is apt to combine with low airspeed to make control indecisive and aircraft response poor. 'Low, slow and downwind' is therefore a condition to be avoided like the plague. So, do not go too far downwind on your overhead

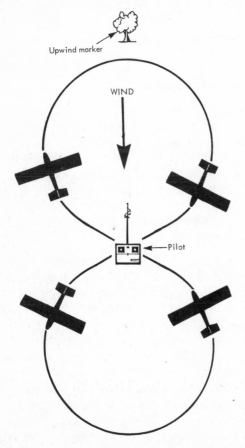

Upwind marker

WIND

Pilot

Fig. 6.4 Overhead eights – practice during quiet periods.

8s; keep plenty of height in hand, and do not let the airspeed fall off as you go belting away down the wind.

This stage need not be continued for more than two or three sessions but be sure that you can reverse a disorientated command quickly and can confidently restrain your model from straying too far downwind.

Stage 4
Climbing, gliding and stalling

It is as well to re-read the Theory of Flight section before tackling this stage. Keep firmly in mind the following principles:—

The model is designed to fly at one speed.
Throttle controls height.
Elevator controls speed.

Using the Upwind Eight pattern, open the throttle and make some climbing 8s. Trim the aircraft to fly hands off, climbing at steady speed and heading. Note any trim adjustments to the climbing attitude of the aircraft. Throttle back to a fast tick-over, re-trim if necessary, and make some descending 8s. Again note trim adjustments and the gliding attitude.

Climb back to a good height, re-trim to cruising revs, and practise stalling. Keeping the aircraft straight with rudder, gently and progressively feed in elevator until the aircraft is flying very slowly in a nose-up attitude. Note the signs of an incipient stall:—

(i) Wallowing, nose-up attitude.
(ii) Progressive loss of control response.
(iii) Sudden dropping of the nose.
(iv) Any tendency (unlikely) to drop a wing.

After the nose has dropped, ease the model out of the dive. (A rude snatch at the elevator might cause another stall, even with the nose right down). Climb again and try one or two more, at different throttle settings. Note how a little throttle will delay the stall.

Trim for descent, and try stalling in a gliding turn. (This is what may happen on a landing approach, when turning onto Base Leg or Finals). Note the attitude of the model as she breaks away, and (probably) the dropping of the 'inside' wing. Recover with rudder, elevator and throttle in that order.

To round off the exercise, get your Instructor to see if the model will spin. (Some trainers won't, but most can be coaxed into it). A spin is a powerful demonstration of what can happen when the aircraft is yawed violently at low speed. If it happens near the ground, there's no chance of recovery.

This is a long exercise, requiring concentration, and rest between flights is desirable. While relaxing, consider the trimming of your aircraft, with frequent reference to the Theory of Flight notes in Chapter 3.

Ideally, the aircraft is built true, with no warps, has perfect lateral balance and the CG precisely where it should be. The angles of incidence of wing and tailplane, and the thrust angles, down and right, of the motor, are exactly as they should be. We have not bolted on anything which produces asymmetric drag; the wheels are perfectly aligned fore and aft—in short, it's an ideal aircraft.

Therefore, provided that we climb, glide and cruise it at the design airspeed, the ideal model will require no trimming. If, like ours, the model is just reasonably well built and rigged, the trim changes required will be hardly perceptible. If you find you are needing a lot of trim, seek expert help or refer to Chapter 7 for advice on corrections. Because once you start on circuit flying things are going to happen quickly, and the last thing you'll need is to be fiddling with the trims.

Stage 5
Taking off

After the usual checks, take out the model and:—

1. Choose a landmark at least 100 yards directly upwind, as an Upwind Marker.
2. Position the model dead into wind,

Take-offs can be tricky with a 'tail-dragger' model as it may tend to swing during the take-off and require sensitive control of the rudder.

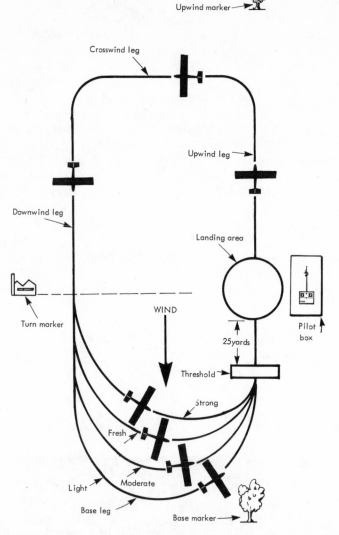

Fig. 6.5 Length of downward leg should be adjusted according to the wind strength; do not go too far downwind when the wind is strong.

Upwind marker →

Crosswind leg

Upwind leg →

Downwind leg →

Landing area

Turn marker

WIND

Pilot box

25 yards

Threshold →

Strong

Fresh

Moderate

Light

Base leg →

Base marker →

held back by a helper.

3. Run up the engine, check the controls at full throttle, return to idle, and ask the helper to stand clear. (A push doesn't help much—do it properly from the beginning!). You should be standing well back from the model yourself in the pilot's box!

4. Open the throttle firmly. As she moves away, there may be an initial swing, probably to the left. Correct this with rudder; it will need more movement than you've been accustomed to using in the air. Once this is

corrected, the aircraft will be picking up speed and will become much more sensitive to rudder. Do not use any more rudder correction.

5. Chop throttle immediately if a bad swing develops (i.e. if you get more than say 20° away from the line of the Marker), or if the motor falters or loses revs (it is almost certainly too lean).

6. Once she's moving smartly along (you'll have seen her take off enough times by now, to be able to judge the moment) come back very gently on

Aim to carry out a low fly past before committing yourself to a landing; it will give you an idea of the correct approach.

the stick until she breaks ground. Watch the attitude carefully, and if the nose comes up too high (i.e. if you continue to see the top of the wing) let the elevator return gently to neutral. Keep her climbing straight towards the Marker. If she climbs steeply, don't panic and start pumping elevator. Your Instructor will have checked her out, and at full throttle a trainer has a wide choice of climbing attitudes. You shouldn't need any down elevator—at neutral she will soon sort herself out.

If you have to clear an obstacle the best way is to let her pick up speed before you try to climb steeply or to turn. 'Hanging on the prop' is no good; the aircraft won't climb, and you may well get a disastrous stall.

Stage 6
Circuit practice

Try to carry out Stages 6–8 at off-peak times, to avoid the distractions of busy traffic in the circuit.

In Stage 6, we shall be making our circuits at constant height, without descending on the final approach. The novice will naturally tend to fly rather too high at first, but he should try to come down as the exercise becomes more familiar, to a comfortable circuit height. Higher circuits are of course safer, but they are much more difficult to fly accurately—and accuracy is now the name of the game.

The diagram on the opposite page is self-explanatory. About six or eight circuits—one or, perhaps, two sessions —should be enough to achieve a fair degree of accuracy. Points to watch:–

Make sure you have clearly identified your Markers.
Make your turns without gaining or losing height.
Don't drift inwards coming downwind.
Check your base-leg turn against the Marker, and regulate the turn so that you arrive above the threshold flying straight and in line with the base Marker. When you can do this every time, you're ready for Stage 7.

45

As the speed of the model decays towards the stalling speed, ease back on the elevator stick and, if you have all the ingredients right, the model will touch down in a three-point attitude.

Stage 7
Practice approaches

Make sure the motor is running well, and will pick up reliably from idling revs, after a prolonged slow run with the nose held slightly down.

Make a circuit as before, but as you go into the Base-Leg turn throttle back to a fast tick-over. Let the nose drop to maintain airspeed, but try to make this turn as before, looking out for the Base Marker.

Once you are in line with the marker, or have got down to about 20 feet, open the throttle and climb away, lining up in due course with the Upwind Marker. On reaching circuit height, throttle back to cruising revs and try again.

After a few attempts you should be able to achieve a correct position over the threshold:—

In line with the Marker
Wings level
15–25 feet up (the more wind, the higher)
Attitude steady, slightly nose down.

When you can do this three times out of three, it's time to try a landing. But don't make up your mind too hastily; be mentally prepared and have the Stage 8 instructions firmly in mind before you come down that last 20 feet.

Stage 8
Landing

Make up your mind that you are only going to land if you achieve a good final approach; if the approach is at all dodgy, you're going to open the throttle fully and go round again. If all is well over the threshold, nothing much can go wrong; in fact, if you chopped the throttle and did nothing more, in all proability she'd get down without damage on her own. So the watchword is, don't overcontrol. We expect you to smooth things out with a little up elevator, but remember:—

Too little is safer than too much
Too late is safer than too soon
As the aircraft passes the threshold she's in her nose-down gliding attitude, with a modicum of throttle, which we now

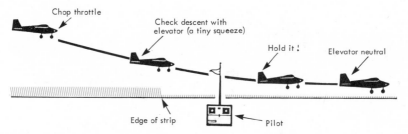

Chop throttle

Check descent with
elevator (a tiny squeeze)

Hold it !

Elevator neutral

Edge of strip

Pilot

Fig. 6.6 The ideal landing approach.

chop. Keep her straight and let her come on down.

At about three feet off the ground gently ease on a little up elevator.

If the nose lifts easily she's too fast—hold the stick where it is, and wait. If the nose is reluctant to come up, she's close to stalling speed, and you can add more up.

BUT REMEMBER—if you use too little elevator, nothing much can go wrong. If you use too much and balloon her, you can do a lot of damage. In a perfect landing, she'll touch down just on the stall, main wheels first—but we don't need a perfect landing, just a safe one.

When she touches, let the stick go to neutral. If there's a little bounce do nothing, and let her sort it out. If there's a big bounce (more than three feet high) bang open the throttle and climb away, but not too steeply.

When she comes to rest, use the throttle trim to cut the motor, hand the Tx to the Instructor, and very calmly retrieve the model. This is the finest moment in all flying, so savour it. Afterwards, you may thank your Instructor and celebrate appropriately!

Stage 9
Forced landings

Everyone has an engine cut now and then. You should practise gliding home

Judging the landing flare only comes with experience; touching down a little fast will not do any harm.

from various points in the sky. Getting into the landing circuit is not the highest priority; you ought to have safety uppermost in your mind. The following precepts may help:—

Decide your plan of action, then make a positive turn.

Keep up the airspeed throughout the glide, and add a bit for turns.

Whatever you do, keep the model in front of you, clear of the pit area and spectators.

Don't continue any turn below 20 feet.

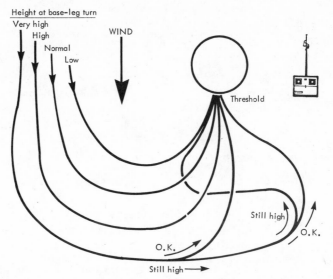

Fig. 6.7 You can adjust the final landing approach turn to compensate for having the model too high or too low.

If that means you have to land downwind, or crosswind, do so; it's safer than putting in a wing-tip.

To practise, climb fairly high, and throttle back. The aim is to get from where you are to the Base-Leg Turn position, arriving from the Downwind Leg at a little above circuit height. Circle overhead until you are at about twice circuit height and then carry out a normal (though descending) circuit. Make your Base Leg so that you feel you'll over-shoot, if anything. The drawing shows how you can vary your approach path, to give you the correct Threshold position. Open up when you arrive there, or before if you get into a mess.

Of course, your engine can cut when you are too low to make it to the Base-Leg Turn position at a decent height. Alas, there are too many possible pos-itions to be itemised in these Notes—most of them are unpleasant, and we do not recommend that you practise them. Try however, to keep in mind the precepts set out above. Whenever you get a low cut you need a little luck, as well as judgement, to get down safely. To reduce the chances of engine cuts, two points:—

Always aim to land with fuel to spare

Don't run your engine weak—after tweaking up to max revs, always open the needle-valve a few notches to be on the safe side.

When you get a genuine cut, call out 'LANDING: DEAD STICK' to warn other fliers.

Stage 10
Primary aerobatics

The manoeuvres suggested here are all within the repertoire of a 3-channel primary trainer, though some only just! Before you start, make sure the aircraft is in good fettle, and you have plenty of bands on the wing. Get some tips, and if possible a demonstration on your model, from your Instructor.

As to the model:—

(i) Increase the control throws, especially rudder; just a little now!
(ii) Make small adjustments to the CG (back 1/4in.) and the wing incidence (1/16in. packing under the trailing edge). You might find you can increase these later, but always go a little at a time
(iii) Make sure the motor is in good form, and won't cut when you shake the model about, point it straight up or down, or invert it.

Before you take off, identify your aerobatic track (see diagram). Some clubs do not regard the use of an aerobatic area as compulsory, but there are good reasons for using one:—

'Aimless' flying does not encourage one to develop well-formed manoeuvres, one needs a constant frame of reference. It is vital when flying aerobatics to keep well clear of the circuit and the pit area.

Should you ever get involved in competition aerobatics, a habitual basic discipline will stand you in good stead.

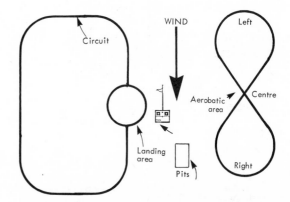

Fig. 6.8 Ideally you should use a separately allocated area, away from the circuit, for aerobatic flying.

Fig. 6.9 Wing over – reversing direction of the model.

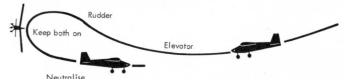

Wing over

This is an easy manoeuvre to begin with. To get the best out of it, make sure you have all the speed you can get, and get that turn really vertical. Keep the dive out fairly shallow, and keep full throttle on throughout, to arrive back at the centre point going flat out, ready for the next manoeuvre. When used as a manoeuvre to join the landing circuit on the crosswind leg, throttle back as you roll out of the vertical turn.

Loops

Loops are also easy to do, but difficult to do well. A good loop is as large as the aircraft can manage, and of perfect circular shape. Because of the large variation in speed a trainer will tend to wander off course; she'll need concentration to keep the wings level. Start with a shallow dive at full throttle to gain maximum speed, and pull up smoothly. To maintain the radius you will probably find you need a little more elevator as she goes through the vertical position, and a little less as she goes over the top. Once you are well over, throttle back, and half-way down ease in a little elevator.

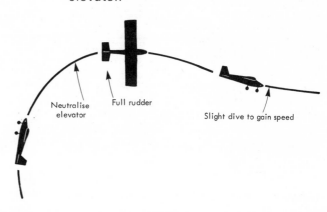

Fig. 6.10 Roll-off-the-top.

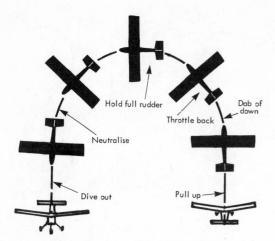

Fig. 6.11 Stall turn – a very satisfying manoeuvre.

Immelmann, or roll-off-the-top

This manoeuvre is only possible because the trainer, with its generous dihedral, is unstable in the rolling plane when inverted. But she will not do it elegantly, and will only oblige if you enter the loop at top speed and keep sufficient speed on over the top to make the rudder effective. Keep full throttle on throughout, and for the best result make the roll to the left. Practise until you know the minimum speed that will give you a tidy exit.

Stall turn

After a quarter-loop, push elevator to maintain a vertical climb, throttle back to 1/3, and as the speed falls off slam on full rudder, yawing the almost stationary aircraft through 180°. Neutralise controls, dive and pull out in the opposite direction.

Ideally, in this pretty manoeuvre, the aircraft virtually pivots about its vertical axis, turning on its own length. In practice, if the airspeed is zero and the throttle closed (no slipstream) the rudder will provide no yawing force, so we have to keep on some airspeed and some throttle to make a positive manoeuvre.

Further, in our trainer, the dihedral introduces a rolling force when we yaw, so that the symmetry of the turn is spoiled. Nevertheless we can make a fair stab at it, especially when we go to the right, when the torque is counteracting the roll. In the writer's view, the Stall Turn is the most rewarding manoeuvre one can do with a 3-channel model, and it is certainly worth a bit of practice to get it right.

Reversal

A simple but exciting manoeuvre, which will bring your model as near to its terminal velocity as anyone wants to get. Start high, keep full throttle until the vertically down position and don't pull too much 'G' on the way out!

Spinning

Learn the difference between a spin and a spiral dive. A Spin is a stalled flick manoeuvre; the aircraft does not circle but spins, nose down, about its vertical axis and autorotates.

From cruising, throttle back and gently pull up the nose. Keep straight with rudder and hold the nose up with more and more elevator. When you have full up, watch for the nose to drop in a stall, and as it falls away bang in full left

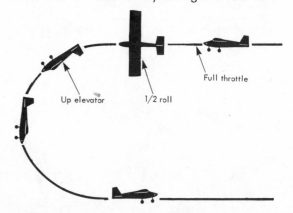

Fig. 6.12 Reversal – start with plenty of height.

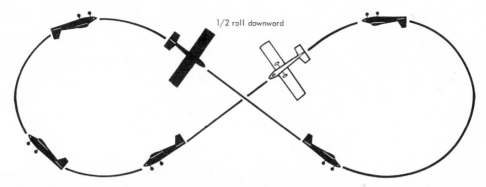

Fig. 6.13 Cuban eight – flown properly it is a very elegant manoeuvre.

rudder. If you've timed it right (and if the CG is far enough back) she'll spin—a sight terrible to behold but perfectly safe with this type of model.

To recover, simply let go the stick—she'll only continue spinning so long as you hold on full rudder and elevator. She comes out in a dive—the airspeed will be low, so beware of pulling out too quickly.

Cuban eight

This makes further use of the trainer's ability to roll out of the inverted position. It calls for a certain sportiness, both from model and pilot; if either is reluctant, put it off until the advent of an aileron model.

Use full throttle throughout.

Start as for Roll-off-the-top, but delay the half-roll until you are diving at 30°. Check the loop with a dab of down, use full rudder and roll upright. Continue diving into the second loop and repeat the delayed roll-off, aiming at a regular 8-shape. Remember to keep plenty of height in hand for this manoeuvre. If you get into trouble, abandon the manoeuvre. Don't try to loop out of an inverted position; always roll; and remember that a little down elevator will pull you out of an inverted dive.

Typical of an aileron trainer, or sports model, the 'Acrocat' will perform all but the most demanding of aerobatics.

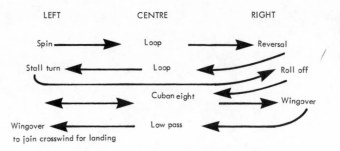

Fig. 6.14 Combining aerobatic manoeuvres into one continuous sequence.

Chain manoeuvres

Now you're a proficient aerobat you may want to think about putting on a show, even if only to entertain yourself. By linking the manoeuvres up and down the track you can achieve something of grace, excitement and interest, even though your aircraft is a mere primary trainer. The diagram overleaf suggests a possible pattern.

Stage 11
Right-hand circuits

Sooner or later, as we remarked before, you will come across a situation which requires a right-hand circuit. The depth of one's incompetence at this can be quite a nasty shock after a long time flying only to the left.

So, when you find yourself alone, try making some right-handers.

That's about all we can do with our Primary Trainer. It's true that we haven't suggested Rolls or Inverted Flight; you might manage to bully your trainer into doing them but she ain't built for that and will never do it gracefully.

If you really feel you've got all you can out of the old dear, you'll be thinking about your next model, or perhaps about making a new aileron wing for Old Faithful. Don't make the decision too early. Use your experience with the Primary to find out what will interest you in the next phase. Do you want more and better aerobatics—more speed and power—or would you rather quietly develop your skill and precision with a more sensitive instrument? You might like to start thinking about STOL, with lots of slottery and flappery, or dropping parachutes and things, or seaplaning, or camera carrying. Do you want a bigger aircraft, for instance? Think about what you've enjoyed most so far, and choose accordingly.

Chapter 7
Trimming the model

Having a correctly trimmed model is vitally important if we are to make flying training as painless and rewarding as it should be. As previously stated, the model can only be perfectly trimmed for one flying speed, but we can reduce the effects of increases or decreases of speeds and the propeller torque.

There are three methods of trimming a model, i.e. of adjusting the forces so that it will fly 'hands off':—

a) *In flight* by using the trim levers on the transmitter to compensate for any aberration. This is strictly a temporary measure, and should be followed by an appropriate adjustment to the control neutrals immediately on landing.

b) *Between flights* by adjusting neutrals. This is still not a final solution; a model should not be flown persistently with offset controls, as the offset effect will be appropriate only at one airspeed.

c) *Permanently* This requires a little patience, but is rewarding both in satisfaction and in flying pleasure. First check out the airframe as follows:—
   1) Check that all control surfaces are free but without slop. If they won't

centre accurately, the plane will never fly true.
2) Make sure that assembly is the same way every time. If you're using rubber bands to hold the wing on, then mark the wing and fuselage (e.g. with auto trim tape) to make sure the wing is always central and square. If you don't it will still fly, but it will fly differently every time you put it together. A good way to check out squareness is to place the model on flagstones and align the flying surfaces with the joints.
3) Make sure the fin is square to the stabiliser, and that the stabiliser is level to the wings. If the stab is high on one side, the model will screw in loops.
4) Get the balance point exactly right. It's important to get the left/right balance point dead-centre on the mid-span of the wings. Otherwise, it will never fly straight at more than one speed, and it will always try to roll out of inverted flight. Suspend the model using thread tied to a pin stuck in the top of the rudder, and with the other end tied to a hook fixed temporarily to the nose centre-line using rubber bands round the fuselage: it's easier to do than to describe, but it will hang freely. To

achieve balance, put woodscrews direct into the tip of the foam wing: they seem to stay there OK.

Once the four basics are right, you take the plane up and trim it in the air. Here you will set the control surface throws and trims as well as fine-tuning the balance. Here is a fault finding chart to confirm whether the former checks have been correctly applied and to assess the engine thrust line. (For a high wing model).

have checked on the ground: balance and trueness. It's easy:

1) First you check the side-to-side balance. The best way to do this is to trim the plane out, and then roll it inverted. You will need to feed in down-elevator to keep it level, but you should not need to feed in any aileron control. If you do, it is because the balance is not right. If you need to feed in right aileron, it's because the right wing is heavy, and

FAULT	ADJUSTMENT
Tail-heavy	
a) Over-responsive to elevator?	Yes Move CG forward 1/4 in No Pack up wing Trailing Edge 1/16 in.
b) Only when throttle open Only when throttle closed	Increase downthrust 1° Reduce downthrust 1°
Nose-heavy	
a) Responds well to elevator?	Yes Pack up wing Leading Edge 1/16 in. No Move CG back 1/4 in.
b) Only when throttle open Only when throttle closed	Reduce downthrust 1° Increase downthrust 1°
Turning tendency	
a) Goes sharp left at full throttle Goes right at full throttle	Increase right thrust 1° Reduce right thrust 1°
b) Needs permanent trim, always the same way	Check for wing warp, tailplane warp, misalignment of wing, tailplane or fin, or nosewheel.
c) Drops wing in stalls, screws out of loops, but not a) or b)	Check lateral balance, and correct by weighting one wing-tip.

When you progress to an aileron equipped aerobatic trainer further checks will be required as follows:

When you've got the model off the ground, and got the general feel of it, trim it on elevator and aileron until it flies straight and level on full throttle. Then fly it around a bit until you have decided that the control throws are OK—not too twitchy and yet with plenty of 'zap'. If you aren't happy, it's better to get the throws right before you go any further. Now you check out in the air all the things you

vice-versa if you need to feed in left aileron. Bring it down and again use small wood-screws to get the balance just right.

2) When the side-to-side balance is right then adjust the rudder trim to compensate for any thrust-line offset. This is easy. On full throttle with wings level, pull steeply into a vertical climb (and then neutralise the stick).

As the plane is now correctly balanced, it should climb steeply without noticeable roll and without falling off to left or right. If it falls off to the left, feed in a little right rudder trim and re-trim the aileron (it may not need changing). Try again, and this time if it falls off to one side, use rudder to get it climbing straight. Keep doing this and altering the trim until it will pull up straight from level flight. When you have got it right it is a good idea to check aileron trim again both upright and inverted. When you have finished steps 1 and 2 your plane should fly straight on the same rudder and aileron trim at all speeds and either way up, provided the tailplane is on straight and the engine is pointing to the front!

3) If you find it hard to get it right, and the plane tries to pull over as it starts to climb but then climbs fairly straight, then this is probably because the wings are not level to the tail: check this before you go any further.

4) When you have set the plane up so that it will pull up straight, look at the set of the rudder with the sticks at neutral. If you have a lot of trim on and the rudder is offset a lot, then the engine thrustline is probably offset. If the rudder trim is set to yaw the plane to the right, then pack the engine mount to make it point to the right.

5) Finally, it's time to check the fore-and-aft balance again. Your trainer will have been trimmed to be speed-stable. It will have been nose-heavy, and the tailplane will have been set to give a down-force. You will probably want to set your new plane up the same to start with. When you are used to it, you will want to make it less speed-stable, and more neutral.

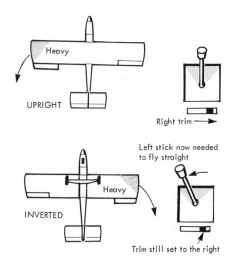

Fig. 7.1 Check the rudder trims by climbing vertically and then re-check aileron trim upright and inverted.

This is easy to do; simply move the centre of gravity back a few millimetres at a time, until it's right. Note that every time you move it back, you increase the power of the elevator, so you may wish to attach the pushrod clevis further out on the elevator horn. You will find it easy to tell when it's right. If you roll the plane inverted at full speed, it will then need very little down-stick to keep it level. Remember that it will be more tail-heavy when the fuel tank is empty, so do your checks with a fairly empty tank, or you will suddenly find it hard to control the first time to fly it nearly dry, e.g. when landing.

If you follow this recipe you will end up with a model that flies where you point it, and which doesn't wander off line. That's what you need to start to learn to fly aerobatic manoeuvres accurately, and that, after all, is what your new plane will be for!

Chapter 8
From trainers to the future

So now you are a fully fledged pilot and are looking for new challenges and flights of fancy. Almost literally, the 'sky is the limit'. There are so many R/C model aircraft avenues to explore that it would take a book—and a very large book—to describe them all in any reasonable detail.

However, we can take a brief look at some of the types of R/C model you can now progress onto, with your newly acquired skills. As with the training models, it is a matter of making steady progress. Don't expect to become an expert in any of the different disciplines of R/C model aircraft overnight, and don't select the most difficult projects immediately. Take your pleasures slowly, increase your experience steadily, but always aim to improve your building and flying standards with each successive model.

Scale

To many modellers scale is the ultimate goal of R/C flying models. This attitude is obvious even at the earliest stages when the budding R/C flier is only interested in a trainer model that resembles a full-size aircraft—even though it may only have a painted cabin to give this illusion. Many a good trainer kit has fallen by the

wayside simply because it was a non-descript design of totally non-scale appearance.

There are, of course, tens of thousands of aircraft prototypes to choose from, but certain types remain firm favourites. Probably the all-time favourite is the Supermarine 'Spitfire', one of the most beautiful aircraft ever designed, and this is a pity because it is not only difficult to build, it also needs considerable skills to fly safely. Fortunately there are other popular subjects that lend themselves far more to the inexperienced scale modeller. The Piper 'Cub', Cessnas, Austers and similar high wing cabin models are an excellent introduction to scale R/C. Many of the light and ultralight subjects make good scale models and plans and kits of them are freely available.

If you must go for the WW2 type fighters, then the N.A. 'Mustang' or the Hawker 'Hurricane' offer a better chance of success than the 'Spitfire'. Still insistent that you want to build a 'Spit'? Well, at least select one of the later marks with the longer noses and increased fin and rudder areas and don't build too small.

Biplanes need not be difficult to fly, particularly some of the earlier examples such as the Sopwith 'Pup', Nieuport 17 or many of the De Havilland 'Moth'

Scale models offer a tremendously wide field of designs – anything from an early 'Bleriot' to one of the latest B2 Stealth bombers – if you can find enough information on the prototype!

series. Please leave the Pitts and Christen Eagles until you have quite a few scale models 'under your belt'.

Multi-engined models can be tricky to fly, the more so if you don't have 100% reliable engines—and no piece of machinery is ever 100% reliable. When you feel sufficiently proficient to move into this exciting area select a design, scale or semi-scale, with the engines close in to the fuselage (to minimise asymmetric thrust problems) parallel chord or moderately tapered wing planform and generous tail areas. The 'Mosquitos' and 'Tigercats' are strictly for the 'macho' men.

With scale models it pays to go to as large a scale as you can cope with—from the economic, transport and storage considerations. Larger models, in general, fly better, it is easier to add scale detail without finishing up with a ridiculously high wing loading and the model also looks more impressive. Do not, however, go beyond your limits of structural experience and move up very cautiously.

Gliders

A whole new world of flying! There are thermal soarers, launched from flat ground, and relying on thermals (uprising warm air currents) to keep them aloft; slope soarers, launched from the side of a hill and relying on the up-currents from the hill to allow them to soar high in the sky. There are scale gliders, pylon racers, competition multi-task sailplanes, aerobatic designs, hand-launch models, all capable of providing fun or competitive excitement. For those of you who hanker for quiet and clean models, gliders are

Powered gliders can be flown with simple two-function radio control equipment and offer an inexpensive entry to the hobby.

There comes a time when you become just a little over confident. If you are lucky you get away with a fright, unlucky and you break a model.

one of the options open to you. In between gliders and standard power models are powered gliders. These are sailplanes (same thing as gliders—it just sounds a little more upmarket) with a power pod fitted over the wing, or sometimes in the nose, so that the model can make its own way to height and not have to rely on a towline, bungee or air currents. Once the motor cuts the model behaves much like a normal sailplane.

Aerobatics

You don't have to enter competitions to enjoy the excitement of high performance aerobatics, although many modellers get an extra 'kick' from participating in a trial of skills. Competition aerobatic models are usually '60' powered (although the large four-stroke engines are now rapidly making their mark) sleek, fast and take up a lot of sky during their manoeuvres. They are not difficult to fly, the art comes in flying them precisely and performing accurate manoeuvres—repeatedly.

Non-competition aerobatic models do not have to be large, you can have a ball flying '20' or '40' powered models. They will be capable of performing most of the manoeuvres of their larger brothers but, from a judging point of view, they

Vintage models are one of the major growth areas in R/C aeromodelling – probably because of a mixture of practical and leisurely flying, together with a little nostalgia.

wouldn't be so impressive or as easy to judge accurately.

Flying aerobatic models is an excellent grounding for any form of R/C flying. It gets you used to co-ordinating all the transmitter controls and having the model in every conceivable attitude, and gives you the confidence to cope with unusual situations—something that can happen with any form of model and, boy, you'd better be ready to react quickly!

Vintage

One of the fastest growing disciplines in R/C aircraft is the Vintage movement. This may be surprising because not all of the fliers of these pre-1951 (many of them pre-1939) aeroplanes can remember the designs the first time round. The nostalgia appeal strikes the young as well as the old. Why? Many of these 'oldie' designs have a definite charm and beauty due to their construction. These are not your veneered foam and GRP models, they have open structure, light but surprisingly strong, and give that ethereal beauty as the sun shines through the covering and exposes the framework.

Slow flying and stable, the vintage models are the complete antithesis of the aerobatic models. These are the types to take out for a relaxing Sunday afternoon's flying.

Floatplanes and flying boats

Flying from water definitely adds another dimension to your hobby; to watch a floatplane lift off a calm surface and trail a fine mist of droplets from the floats is a delightful sight. Equally satisfying is a landing where the model alights on the water and settles slowly into its water-borne state. Certainly, there is a little more construction work with a floatplane or flying boat and some additional precautions required to make the plane watertight, but it is all worthwhile.

There are a surprising number of inland water sites in the country, not all with sole rights owned by fishermen, so why not give this novel form of flying a go?

Pylon racing

For real adrenalin-producing excitement there is little to beat pylon racing. With

Flying off water adds a whole new dimension; there are flying boat and float-plane kits and plans available.

models attaining speeds of 125mph (Club 20 racing) and 150mph plus (FAI racers) it calls for a cool nerve and good reactions as four models power their way round a triangular course. Obviously, with speeds of this order, and flying relatively close to the ground, you have to be a fairly competent pilot to enter the racing circuit. However, Club 20 or *Quickie 500* pylon racers are pleasant to fly and once you have become accustomed to the extra speed you will find them no more difficult to control than an aerobatic model. They also have good slow speed characteristics when fitted with a throttle control.

Electric powered models

Gaining respectability at last, thanks to great improvements in motors, batteries, propellers and model design, electric powered models are now a very practical proposition. No longer confined to the 'powered glider' type of model, electric power is now used for aerobatic designs, single and multi-engined scale models and there is a whole range of 'almost-ready-to-fly' designs on the market.

Blessed with near silence and next-to-nothing running costs, electric power could turn out to be the saviour of our hobby by allowing us to fly again in public places—without annoying the public.

Sports models

These cover a wide spectrum that are intended for fun flying rather than for a particular aspect of R/C flying. Models range from 'flying saucers' to deltas, canards, biplanes and triplanes or simple semi-scale cabin models. The permutations of sizes and shapes are endless and there is no reason why you shouldn't have a go at designing one yourself. Take a standard well-established design. modify it in shape (but keeping to the general areas and moments) and you are half way to being a model aeroplane designer! With a little more experience you will find yourself starting from a plain sheet of paper and finishing up with an entirely new creation.

Ducted fan models

Apart from pulse jets (nasty, fire breathing engines) the only practical way of simulating scale gas turbine powered aircraft is by using ducted fan units. Instead of having a propeller fitted on the front of the model, the engine is mounted amidships in the fuselage (in a duct) and a multi-bladed fan is fitted to the engine. Although less efficient than propellers, well-designed fan units, allied to extremely powerful engines, are capable of propelling scale jet models at well in excess of 100mph. This form of propulsion opens up many prototypes that could not previously be modelled—without cheating and putting a propeller on the front, or rear.

Large models

Throughout the world there has been a tremendous increase in the building and flying of large models, nearly all of them of scale subjects. Enormous models spanning over twenty feet, weighing hundreds of pounds and powered by engines of up to 400cc have been successfully flown (a man-carrying microlight aircraft was recently modified for R/C operation in Australia!). As stated previously, large scale models fly well and look majestic in the air; they have a reality that few of the small models can match.

Operating these jumbo models brings with it a lot of responsibility. Structural integrity is vital with these miniature aircraft, which are potentially more dangerous unless constructed correctly and flown in a responsible manner.

Simulation of jet motors is carried out by using ducted fan units, ie. high performance two-stroke engines, operating at over 20,000 rpm, and multi-bladed fan assemblies. These units operate in an internal duct.

Before entering into this exciting phase of R/C modelling you will need to build up gradually to the larger types and to have expert guidance from specialised associations. There may be government legislation restricting the flying of these giants.

Helicopters

Last, but by no means least, is the alternative form of R/C flying—helicopters. These rotary wing masterpieces of engineering require a different approach to flying compared with the fixed wing aeroplanes. Not the easiest of models to learn to fly (it has been compared to balancing two poles on your hands—with your arms crossed) the sense of satisfaction in being able to accurately hover a helicopter is great indeed. Gradual improvements to helicopter design has brought about kits that are easy to assemble accurately and the use of gyros and sophisticated transmitters certainly makes helicopter flying a much better proposition than it was a few years ago. Any modeller with a reasonable degree of perseverance and normal reactions should be able to master helicopter flying within a few months.

And on . . . and on . . . and on . . .

Yes, the permutations of R/C model aircraft building and flying are almost endless. We haven't even mentioned autogyros or camera-carrying models—or parachute dropping—or flexiwings or . . . pulse jets—or . . .

Appendix

Check lists

Regular inspections of the model, engine and radio equipment—and the field box—will help to ensure reliable flying and longevity for the model. Preparation for the flying field was discussed and a check list given on page 31; here are the other essential checks.

Evening inspection before flying

Security of motor plate, engine and silencer bolts, carb. body, plug. Propeller nut tight; spinner secure. Condition of propeller and spinner. Tank airtight, clunk secure, feed vent lines free, hatch secure. Noseleg secure, wheel aligned, free-running, collets tight. Main legs secure, wheels as for nosewheel, soldered joints holding. Ground angle neutral; i.e. model horizontal at rest on ground. Condition of fuselage underside. Tailplane and fin secure, correctly aligned, free of warps. Elevator and rudder hinges secure and free-moving. Horns and clevises secure; push-rod exits free. Fuselage sides and top; condition.

Receiver switch clean and free of oil. Aerial secure, unstrained. Servos securely fitted and vibration-damped; output levers screwed down. Clevises and links secure; pushrods free-running.

Receiver and battery securely stowed and padded. Switch on Tx and Rx. Servos move cleanly with commands; unobstructed full travel; correct centering.

Controls move in the correct sense and with the specified throws. Rudder and elevator neutrals and throttle range correct. Inspect wing for warps and damage. Condition of dowels and wing seating tape. Wing correctly aligned with tailplane. Switch off Tx and Rx, and put on charge. Charge 12v and 2v batteries as required (Flight-box).

Pre-flight checks

Correct pit position in relation to wind direction.
Assemble model; check alignment of flying surfaces.
Fill fuel tank.
Obtain frequency peg or other required clearance.
Radio check; range check if required.
Extend Tx aerial.
Prime motor. Before starting, check that nothing critical (e.g. maiden flight or first solo) is going on.
Start motor; tune for full throttle; nose-up check.
Slow-running and control checks.
Check no aircraft in landing pattern.

Take-off checks

Re-check frequency peg
No aircraft on finals
Carry the model out, and align into wind
Run-up and control checks
Remove yourself promptly from the landing path to the pilots' box.
Final check for aircraft on the approach
Take off.

After flight

Remove model promptly from the landing area
Switch off Rx and Tx. Collapse Tx aerial.
Return frequency peg.
Heavy landing check;
   Undercarriage, fuselage bottom
   (from nose-leg) wing alignment,
   tailplane and fin security, propeller for
    damage
   Wipe down fuel-soiled areas.

Index

Subscribe now...

here's 4 good reasons why!

Within each issue these four informative magazines provide the expertise, advice and inspiration you need to keep abreast of developments in the exciting field of model aviation.

With regular new designs to build, practical features that take the mysteries out of construction, reports and detailed descriptions of the techniques and ideas of the pioneering aircraft modellers all over the world – they represent four of the very best reasons for taking out a subscription.

You need never miss a single issue or a single minute of aeromodelling pleasure again!

	U.K.	Europe	Middle East	Far East	Rest of World
Aeromodeller *Published monthly*	£23.40	£28.20	£28.40	£30.20	£28.70
Radio Modeller *Published monthly*	£15.60	£21.20	£21.40	£23.60	£21.80
RCM&E *Published monthly*	£15.60	£21.60	£21.80	£24.00	£22.20
Radio Control Scale Aircraft *Published quarterly*	£9.00	£11.10	£11.20	£12.00	£11.30

Your remittance with delivery details should be sent to:

The Subscriptions Manager (CG/15)
Argus Specialist Publications
1 Golden Square LONDON W1R 3AB.